DK State-by-State
ATLAS

DK State-by-State
ATLAS

Justine Ciovacco, Kathleen A. Feeley,
and Kristen Behrens

DK PUBLISHING, INC.

**LONDON, NEW YORK, MUNICH,
MELBOURNE, AND DELHI**

Managing Editor Beth Sutinis
Art Editor Megan Clayton
Editorial Assistant Madeline Farbman
Publisher Chuck Lang
Creative Director Tina Vaughan
Editorial Director Valerie Buckingham
Production Chris Avgherinos

MEDIA PROJECTS INC.
Executive Editor Carter Smith
Project Editor Kristen Behrens
Designer Laura Smyth
Photo Researcher Kristen Behrens
Assistant Photo Researcher James Burmester
Photo Research Assistants Katie Briggs and Céline Geiger

This edition published in the United States in 2006
by DK Publishing, Inc.
375 Hudson Street
New York, NY 10014

09 10 9 8 7 6

DK Publishing, Inc. offers special discounts for bulk purchases for sales promotions or premiums. Specific,
large-quantity needs can be met with special editions, including personalized covers, excerpts of existing
guides, and corporate imprints. For more information, contact Special Markets Department, DK
Publishing, Inc., 375 Hudson Street, New York, NY 10014 Fax: 800-600-9098.

Library of Congress Cataloging-in-Publication Data

Ciovacco, Justine.
    State-by-state atlas / by Justine Ciovacco, Kathleen A. Feeley, and Kristen Behrens.— 1st American ed.
        p. cm.
Includes index.
ISBN-13: 978-0-7566-1828-5
ISBN-10: 0-7566-1828-2
1. United States—Geography—Juvenile literature. 2. United States—Maps for children. 3. U.S. states—
Juvenile literature. [1. United States—Geography. 2. United States—Maps. 3. Atlases.] I. Feeley, Kathleen,
1968- II. Behrens, Kristen. III. Title.

E161.3.C56 2002
912.73—dc21
                        2002154881

Reproduced by Colourscan, Singapore
Printed in China by Toppan Printing Co., (Shenzhen) Ltd.

Discover more at
www.dk.com

CONTENTS

THE UNITED STATES 6

THE NORTHEAST STATES 8

*The Statue
of Liberty*

THE SOUTHEAST STATES 32

Muddy Waters

THE MIDWEST STATES 58

Wheat field

THE PLAINS STATES 76

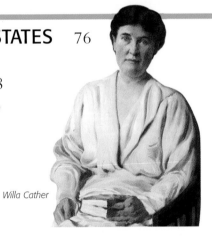

Willa Cather

THE SOUTHWEST STATES 88

Saguaro cactus

Gila monster

THE ROCKY MOUNTAIN STATES 98

Pronghorn

THE PACIFIC STATES 110

Wagon train

WASHINGTON, D.C. AND OUTLYING REGIONS 122

George Washington

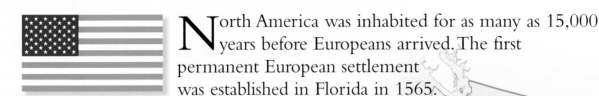

THE UNITED STATES OF AMERICA

Northern America was inhabited for as many as 15,000 years before Europeans arrived. The first permanent European settlement was established in Florida in 1565. 211 years of colonization followed, until the United States was established in 1776. Since then, the nation has grown from 13 states to 50 and spread across the continent. The United States came to symbolize political, economic, and religious freedom for immigrants who arrived from every corner of the world. Today, with a population exceeding 293 million, the U.S. is an international power, leading the world in food production, technological innovation, and more.

ALASKA

HAWAII

WASHINGTON

OREGON

IDAHO

MONTANA

WYOMING

NEVADA

■ Yosemite National Park

UTAH

CALIFORNIA

ARIZONA

PACIFIC OCEAN

COLORA

NEW MEXICO

YOSEMITE NATIONAL PARK
From waterfalls to groves of giant sequoia trees to the flower-filled fields of the Tuolumne meadows, the 761,236 acres (308,072 hectares) of this national park were saved from development primarily through the efforts of environmentalist John Muir, the founder of the Sierra Club. The landscape was formed millions of years ago when glaciers created the path in which the Merced River flows.

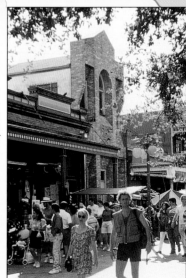

SOUTHWEST STYLE
The Spanish, and later the Mexicans, once held the southwestern regions of what would become the United States. Today the flavor of Latin culture is still present in open-air markets such as this one in San Antonio. Many of the place names in this region can trace their names to Spanish roots, as can many of the people. Thirty-two percent of Texas's population, for example, claims Latino heritage.

GOLDEN CORN
Corn is among the United States' top crops, generating millions of dollars in revenue each year. Much of that corn is grown in the country's center, with Iowa leading in corn production. Corn is used as feed for livestock, but it is also processed into meal, oil, and other products that are shipped throughout the country, and the world.

NEW ENGLAND REGATTA
The Head of the Charles regatta, held in Boston, Massachusetts each year, is just one of New England's events that link the bustling present to the historic past. Boston is a city loaded with colonial history; it was central to the nation's birth during the American Revolution.

NORTH DAKOTA

MINNESOTA

SOUTH DAKOTA

WISCONSIN

Lake Superior

Lake Huron

MICHIGAN

Lake Michigan

Lake Ontario

Lake Erie

NEW HAMPSHIRE

MAINE

VERMONT

NEW YORK

Boston

MASSACHUSETTS

New York City

RHODE ISLAND

NEBRASKA

IOWA

ILLINOIS

INDIANA

OHIO

PENNSYLVANIA

Philadelphia

CONNECTICUT

NEW JERSEY

DELAWARE

MARYLAND

WASHINGTON, D.C.

KANSAS

MISSOURI

WEST VIRGINIA

VIRGINIA

KENTUCKY

OKLAHOMA

ARKANSAS

TENNESSEE

NORTH CAROLINA

SOUTH CAROLINA

TEXAS

MISSISSIPPI

ALABAMA

GEORGIA

ATLANTIC OCEAN

San Antonio

LOUISIANA

Mississippi Delta

Gulf of Mexico

FLORIDA

BIG APPLES
New York City is called the "Big Apple," but not because New York state is a top apple producer—although it is. In the 1920s and 1930s, *apple* was jazz musicians' slang for city—and the biggest apple was NYC.

LIBERTY BELL
Philadelphia, the city of brotherly love, was also central to the United States' birth in 1776. Among the important historic sites are Benjamin Franklin's home; Independence Hall, where the Declaration of Independence was signed; and, of course, the Liberty Bell.

THE MISSISSIPPI DELTA
The Mississippi River takes a roughly 2,300-mile (3,701-km) journey from its source in Minnesota to the Mississippi Delta in Louisiana. Today, as when René-Robert Cavelier, Sieur de La Salle journeyed up the river in 1682, the mighty waterway is a "river road" that reaches from the Great Lakes to the Gulf of Mexico.

THE NORTHEAST STATES

Although Spanish expeditions reached the Northeast's coastline in the 1500s, English, Dutch, and French explorers claimed the region. At that point, American Indians had been living there for as long as 10,000 years. Nine of the 11 Northeast states—Massachusetts, Rhode Island, New Hampshire, Connecticut, New York, New Jersey, Pennsylvania, Delaware, and Maryland—were among the 13 original British colonies. This region was also a center for patriot protest in the years leading up to the American Revolution.

The Statue of Liberty, a 305-foot-high (93 m) statue, was a gift from the French government. Dedicated in 1886, it stands as symbol of welcome to immigrants from around the world. The poem on its pedestal, "The New Colossus" by Emma Lazarus, reads, in part, "Send these, the homeless, tempest-tost to me, I lift my lamp beside the golden door!"

Later, the Northeast was the U.S. Industrial Revolution's birthplace. The port cities of Boston, New York, and Baltimore have long made the region a center for commerce and trade. These cities have also served as gateways for immigrants who continue to contribute to a diverse population and culture.

Outside the region's urban centers is rural land dotted with apple orchards and dairy farms. The Atlantic Coast's rich fishing grounds continue to fuel the region's economy while the area's natural beauty, rich history, and vibrant cities draw visitors year round.

CLIMATE

The region has warm, humid summers and cold, snowy winters. From north to south, there is a wide variation in weather. Maine receives as much as 90 inches (229 cm) of snowfall each year, with an average winter temperature of 22°F (-6°C), while eastern Maryland has a humid subtropical climate and receives relatively little snowfall—its winter temperature average is 35°F (2°C). Coastal regions are also subject to hurricanes and storms called nor'easters, which can cause floods and blizzards. The Adirondack Mountains in New York and the Green Mountains in Vermont are among the Northeast's many mountain ranges. Here weather conditions tend to be colder and windier with peaks that are snow-covered even in early summer.

Autumn in the Northeast brings brilliantly colored foliage in the countryside, which draws many visitors to the region's mountain ranges and river valleys.

KEY DATES

1620 Pilgrims land at Plymouth Rock and establish the first permanent settlement by white people in the Northeast.

1772 A major act of colonial defiance against Great Britain takes place in Rhode Island, where colonists sink the *Gaspee*, a British customs ship.

1787 Delaware is the first state of the original 13 to ratify the new U. S. Constitution. Rhode Island is the last to do so, in 1790.

LANDSCAPE

Glaciers shaped the Northeast's landscape as far south as Long Island, New York, creating mountain chains and river valleys. The region's highest peak, Mt. Washington, lies in New Hampshire. Forests cover much of the land; more than 60 percent of Connecticut is forested, making it an ideal location to enjoy the Northeast's fall foliage. The region's Atlantic coastline is also a source of work and play. The long shoreline changes from the steep rock cliffs of Maine to the sandy beaches of the coastal plain, stretching south to New Jersey and Delaware. The 130-mile (209-km) New Jersey coast is a popular destination for a day at the beach. The Jersey shore also features the boardwalk of Atlantic City and the bright lights of that city's gambling casinos. Commercial fishermen navigate the coastal waters of Maine, Massachusetts, and Delaware, catching lobster in the waters of New England and crab to the south in the Chesapeake Bay.

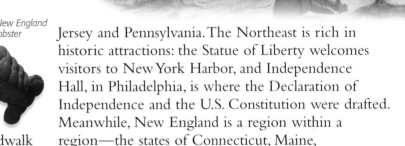

Winslow Homer's painting Maine Fisherman *captures the travails of the commercial fishermen who have worked the waters of the North Atlantic since colonial times.*

New England lobster

Jersey and Pennsylvania. The Northeast is rich in historic attractions: the Statue of Liberty welcomes visitors to New York Harbor, and Independence Hall, in Philadelphia, is where the Declaration of Independence and the U.S. Constitution were drafted. Meanwhile, New England is a region within a region—the states of Connecticut, Maine, Massachusetts, New Hampshire, Rhode Island, and Vermont share the "Yankee" spirit.

ECONOMY

Seaports, always essential to the economy of the Northeast, have thrived through the years because of trade, shipbuilding, and fishing. Maryland's Chesapeake Bay provides much of the nation's blue crab harvest, while lobster is an important catch in New England. Publishing, insurance, and finance companies are found in the Northeast's major cities. A wide variety of agricultural goods are produced, too, including ice cream from Vermont's dairy products. Massachusetts's Cape Cod and the Civil War battlefield at Gettysburg, Pennsylvania, are just a two of the attractions that bring tourist revenue.

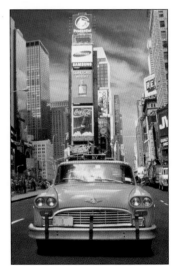

New York City, an international center of finance, commerce, and culture, is the nation's largest city with a population of more than eight million.

Philadelphia's Independence Hall is one of many historic sites in the Northeast from the Revolutionary period. The hall is part of a national park site that also houses the Liberty Bell.

LIFESTYLE

The Northeast includes the hustle and bustle of New York City as well as the natural beauty of the Appalachian Mountains. City dwellers can escape to the Delaware Water Gap, which extends from New

1812 Francis Scott Key writes the nation's anthem after observing the British attack on Fort McHenry, Maryland, during the War of 1812.

1863 The Battle of Gettysburg in Pennsylvania is a key victory for the Union. The war ends following the South's surrender in 1865.

1929 The New York Stock Exchange crashes, ending a period of growth and prosperity and ushering in the Great Depression.

2001 Terrorists attack New York City and Washington, D.C., on September 11, killing more than 3,000 people. New York City's World Trade Center towers collapse.

STATE BIRD
Chickadee

STATE FLOWER
White Pine Cone
and Tassel

STATE TREE
Eastern White Pine

CAPITAL
Augusta

POPULATION
1,274,923 (2000)

STATEHOOD
March 15, 1820
Rank: 23rd

LARGEST CITIES
Portland (64,249)
Lewiston (35,690)
Bangor (31,473)

LAND AREA
30,862 sq. mi.
(79,933 sq. km.)

MAINE
the pine tree state

The Kennebec, Passamaquoddy, and Penobscot were hunting, farming, and fishing in the region when the first waves of European settlers arrived in the 1620s. The state's name came either from a French province or because early European settlers took to calling it the "mainland" to distinguish it from its many coastal islands.

British and French colonists jockeyed for control of the region for more than a century. A young United States finally gained control of Maine at the end of the American Revolution, but both border conflicts with Canada and the issue of statehood remained contentious issues, partially because other states, including Massachusetts, wanted to add Maine's land to their own.

Maine became a state 1820, and its border with Canada was fixed in 1842. The state's natural resources led to strong fishing, shipbuilding, and timber industries that drew settlers throughout the mid-1800s; these industries remain important to the economy. Today's shipbuilding industry has modernized to include nuclear-powered submarines.

Maine enjoys a moderate summer climate with an average temperature of 70°F (21°C). With an average winter temperature of 22°F (–5.6°C) and between 60 and 90 inches (152 and 229 cm) of snow every year, this mountainous state is a popular destination for skiing and other winter sports.

CANADA

Mt. Katahdin ▲

Moosehead Lake

MAINE

WHITE MOUNTAINS

NEW HAMPSHIRE

Bangor ●

AUGUSTA ★

● Lewiston

Rockland ●

Bath ●

Vinalhaven Island

● Portland

● Sanford

Gulf of Maine

● Kennebunkport

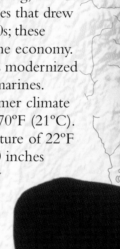

KING PHILIP'S WAR
As British and colonial settlers encroached on American Indian lands, the Wampanoag's leader, King Phillip (known also as Metacom), organized tribal resistance throughout New England. In the summer of 1675, battles broke out that led to the loss of more than 3,500 lives. Most Indians were forced to give up their lands to white settlers and relocate farther north or west.

DID YOU KNOW?
Maine is the only U.S. state with a one-syllable name.

MAJOR MOOSE
Maine is the most heavily forested state in the nation: 17 million acres (6.9 million hectares) of forest cover 90 percent of the state. This makes for abundant and varied wildlife, including beavers, bobcats, coyotes, and porcupine. Maine is home to one of the nation's largest moose populations. An estimated 29,000 moose are found primarily in the state's north. They feast on the state's many trees as well as aquatic plants found in Maine's 6,000 lakes and ponds.

CANADA

Calais

Sail Rock

Milbridge

THE FAR EAST

Jutting out of the frigid waters of the North Atlantic just offshore from the historic West Quoddy Head lighthouse is Sail Rock, considered the easternmost point in the United States. The lighthouse was first built by order of President Thomas Jefferson in 1808 to light the way for sailors navigating Maine's rocky coastline.

LOBSTERFEST

The "lobster capital of the world," Rockland, hosts an annual festival celebrating Maine's maritime heritage. It includes live entertainment; the Crate Race, in which participants try to cross the harbor without falling into the water; and, of course, the eating of tons of lobster.

WEDDING CAKE

The George W. Bourne House, better known as the "Wedding Cake House," is located in the picturesque village and summer resort of Kennebunkport. Originally built in 1826 as a simple brick home, its shipbuilder owner later added the fanciful gingerbread and turrets that have made the building a must-see for tourists.

KING OF HORROR

STEPHEN KING

Portland-born author Stephen King first rose to fame in 1974 with the publication of his first novel, *Carrie*. King has since become a best-selling and beloved author who helped reshape and revive the horror genre. This prolific author, known for his compelling storytelling, writes in a wide range of genres—horror, science fiction, and fantasy—and is a leader in innovative publishing formats, including e-books and serials. Most of his novels and short stories take place in New England.

King intends to retire from publishing his writing after his next few novels are published.

LOBSTER FISHING

Fifty-seven million pounds (25,855,030 kg) of lobster were harvested in Maine in 2000, making this clawed crustacean an important part of the state's economy and culture. The state also has significant natural resources that make outdoor recreation possible in all seasons. This has made the tourism industry important to Maine's economy. Visitors to Maine's many southern coastal resorts enjoy sandy beaches and blue sea for sunning, swimming, sailing, and fishing.

WINDY PEAKS

At 5,268 feet (1,606 m), Mt. Katahdin is Maine's highest point and the northern terminus of the Appalachian National Scenic Trail, a 2,158-mile (3,473 km) hiking path through 14 states. Mount Katahdin is part of the White Mountains, which extend into western and central Maine as well as New Hampshire. Northern and eastern Maine boast river valleys, mountains, and rolling plateaus. More than 1,200 islands are found off of Maine's rugged Atlantic coastline. Many, like Vinalhaven Island, support thriving year-round and summer human populations while others can support only roosting birds.

NEW HAMPSHIRE
the granite state

CANADA

STATE FACTS

STATE BIRD
Purple Finch

STATE FLOWER
Purple Lilac

STATE TREE
White Birch

CAPITAL
Concord

POPULATION
1,235,786 (2000)

STATEHOOD
June 21, 1788
Rank: 9th

LARGEST CITIES
Manchester (107,006)
Nashua (86,605)
Concord (40,687)

LAND AREA
8,968 sq. mi.
(23,227 sq. km.)

Approximately 5,000 American Indians, mostly of the Algonquian family, inhabited the New Hampshire region before Europeans settled there in the early 1600s. In 1603, Englishman Martin Pring explored the area by leading a trading ship up the Piscataqua River.

England's Council for New England began granting land to settlers in the 1620s. Among those given land was Captain John Mason. Mason called the area New Hampshire after his homeland of Hampshire, England. King Charles II of England declared the land to be the province of New Hampshire in 1680.

Hundreds of men from New Hampshire joined the fight against the British in the American Revolution, even though it was the only colony of the original 13 in which no fighting actually occurred.

Today, New Hampshire prides itself on its "Yankee" traditions of self-reliance and independence. Every four years since 1920, it has held the nation's first presidential primary. Primaries are pre-election votes held to narrow the field of presidential hopefuls, and New Hampshire holds its primary in February—nine months ahead of the nation's election day. Between 1952 and 1992, no presidential candidate has won the presidency without first winning the New Hampshire primary.

Dixville Notch

Connecticut River

MAINE

Mt. Washington

WHITE MOUNTAINS

VERMONT

NEW HAMPSHIRE

Connecticut River

Lake Winnipesaukee

CONCORD ★

Manchester

East Derry

America's Stonehenge

New Ipswich

Nashua

MASSACHUSETTS

GROWING WHAT'S NATURAL

New Hampshire's agricultural resources include dairy products, cattle, eggs, and greenhouse plants. Farming is difficult because the state's hills and mountains are rocky and covered with only a thin layer of soil. The rock had its own use, though—granite was once quarried in New Hampshire, which gave the state its best-known nickname, the Granite State. Meanwhile, New Hampshire's soil, filled with clay and loam, creates a strong foundation for trees, which cover almost 85 percent of the state. Milling lumber has been an important part of the state's economy since 1631. Most of the timber cut today is used in paper production.

INDEPENDENT SPIRIT

In politics and economics, the state's people and policies have always shown a strong independent vision and trail-blazing spirit. On January 5, 1776, the state became the first of the 13 original colonies to declare its independence. Today, New Hampshire is known as one of only two states to have no state income tax and no sales tax—policies that residents believe are good for both consumers and businesses.

DID YOU KNOW?

Each primary day, voters in Dixville Notch become the first U.S. citizens to vote for presidential hopefuls. The polling site in the tiny town, population 100, opens at midnight.

AMERICA'S STONEHENGE

Archeologists are unsure exactly who built "America's Stonehenge," which is estimated to be more than 4,000 years old. Near North Salem, it is one of the oldest stone-constructed sites in North America. Tourists also visit the site to hike through the nearby woods. Like England's Stonehenge, it can still be used to determine solar and lunar events.

THE FOUR SEASONS

In fall, colorful foliage lines the country roads of New Hampshire. In winter, the state is covered with a blanket of snow. Each year, the state receives an average of 50 inches (127 cm) of snow, with amounts in the north and west often topping 100 inches (254 cm). The state's climate is cool with the southern half a few degrees warmer than the north. Temperatures in July average 68°F (20°C), while January temperatures hover around 19°F (-7°C).

PAST GLORY IN TEXTILES

In the early 1800s, New Hampshire's manufacturing business boomed. A cotton mill opened in New Ipswich in 1804; six years later, eleven more mills followed. New Hampshire's strong streams turned waterwheels that powered equipment in many preindustrial mills. New Hampshire's mills were also credited with helping Union efforts during the Civil War. Manchester mills turned cotton into cloth for thousands of uniforms.

FIRST AMERICAN IN SPACE

ALAN SHEPARD

Born in East Derry, New Hampshire, Alan Shepard was selected as one of NASA's first astronauts in April 1959. He trained for more than a year before learning that he would make NASA's first space flight. *Freedom 7* was launched on May 5. Shepard flew on a 15-minute sub-orbit above Earth before his capsule splashed down in the Atlantic Ocean. In 1971, Shepard returned to space aboard *Apollo 14*.

Shepard's wartime courage and piloting skills brought him to the attention of NASA officials.

HIGHEST NORTHEASTERN POINT

Mount Washington towers above New Hampshire as the highest point in northeastern United States. At 6,288 feet (1,917 m) in height it's also the windiest place in the country. The strongest winds ever recorded there blew in April 1934, when wind speeds hit 231 miles per hour (372 kph). Mount Washington's summit is usually cloud-capped and often has traces of snow in early summer. The mountain is part of the Presidential Range, a chain of mountains named for U.S. presidents including Monroe, Jefferson, Madison, and Adams. The peaks are part of the White Mountain Range.

STATE FACTS

STATE BIRD
Hermit Thrush

STATE FLOWER
Red Clover

STATE TREE
Sugar Maple

CAPITAL
Montpelier

POPULATION
608,827 (2000)

STATEHOOD
March 4, 1791
Rank: 14th

LARGEST CITIES
Burlington (38,889)
Essex (18,626)
Rutland (17,292)

LAND AREA
9,250 sq. mi.
(23,958 sq. km.)

VERMONT

the green mountain state

The French words *vert*, meaning "green," and *mont*, meaning "mountain," were combined to create Vermont's name and celebrate the mountain range—the Green Mountains—that dominates the state's landscape. When New York and New Hampshire were colonies, they both claimed the land that became Vermont. Meanwhile, Vermont's proximity to Canada via land and water made it strategically important during the American Revolution, as well as the War of 1812.

The Iroquois and Abenaki struggled for control of the land in the 1600s. They drew European allies—the English and the French—into the conflict in the latter half of the century. After much warfare, the English gained control of the region in 1763. Later, neighboring New York and New Hampshire sought to annex Vermont. Finally Vermont became a state in its own right on March 4, 1791. Vermont has a long history of political independence—it is the only state to enter the Union prior to the Civil War with a constitution that prohibited slavery.

The state's agricultural production has been shaped by its largely steep terrain and rocky soil, and dairy farming predominates. Food processing is an important industry, and includes ice cream, cheddar cheese, and maple syrup. Vermont's largely rural lifestyle draws visitors year-round to sample the pleasures of small-town life and enjoy outdoor recreation of all kinds. The state's long, cold, snow-filled winters and considerable number of mountain ranges make skiing the state's most important tourist industry.

Map labels:
North Hero · Enosburg Falls · Saint Albans · Milton · Lake Champlain · Colchester · Essex · Burlington · MONTPELIER · Vergennes · Bristol · VERMONT · GREEN MOUNTAINS · NEW YORK · Rutland · Poultney · Wallingford · Manchester · Stratton Mountain · Arlington · Bennington · MASSACHUSETTS

LAKE CHAMPLAIN

Vermont's many mountain ranges and its northern latitude make for long, cold winters with 70 to 120 inches of snowfall per year. Lake Champlain, in northwestern Vermont, is the state's lowest point, and the surrounding valley has the state's longest growing season, thanks to its low elevations. The lake has a warming effect on the valley.

HERO OF THE REVOLUTION

Allen worked tirelessly to secure statehood for Vermont.

ETHAN ALLEN

Ethan Allen settled in Vermont in 1769 as the colonies of New York and New Hampshire vied for control of the region. The following year Allen organized the Green Mountain Boys, a militia that fought against annexation by New York, and for making the region a separate colony. When the American Revolution began, Allen's Green Mountain Boys took up arms against the British and scored an important victory by capturing Fort Ticonderoga.

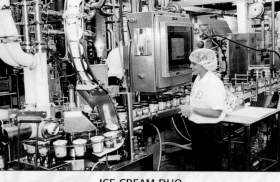

ICE CREAM DUO

Ben & Jerry's was founded in 1978 by Ben Cohen and Jerry Greenfield, who started the business working out of a converted gas station in Burlington, Vermont. Using fresh goods from Vermont's many dairy farms to create unique flavors in innovative packaging, the company's ice cream, sorbet, and frozen yogurt have become national favorites.

MORE MILK, PLEASE!

Vermont farmers raised sheep until competition from western states forced them to look to other agricultural products. The advent of the refrigerated railway car in the mid-1800s was a boon since it meant that it was possible to ship Vermont milk across long distances. From then on, Vermont has been a major milk state, in keeping with the state's rural image.

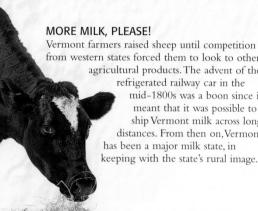

GOING HUGE

Stratton Mountain has hosted the U.S. Open Snowboarding Championships. Vermont's economy relies heavily on tourism, and the winter ski season brings in the most income. The state is an important destination for winter sports enthusiasts of all ages and skill levels. Visitors also travel to Vermont year-round to fish and swim in the state's 300-plus lakes and hike and bike its mountain trails.

DID YOU KNOW?

Vermont granite was used to build the U.S. Supreme Court building in Washington, D.C.

FAMOUS GRANITE

The Rock of Ages granite quarry is one of the world's largest. It, and many others, are found in and around Barre in central Vermont. The city, known as the "Granite Capital of the World," attracted highly skilled stoneworkers from Italy, Spain, and Wales during the 1800s.

MAJOR MAPLE

Vermont's heavily forested woodlands and mountains make it the nation's leading producer of maple syrup and maple sugar, made from the sap of the state's official tree. Maple sap is collected and brought to a sugaring house. There it is boiled and reduced into syrup. It takes 40 gallons (151 l) of sap to make 1 gallon (3.8 l) of syrup!

STATE BIRD
Chickadee

STATE FLOWER
Mayflower

STATE TREE
American Elm

CAPITAL
Boston

POPULATION
6,349,097 (2000)

STATEHOOD
February 6, 1788
Rank: 6th

LARGEST CITIES
Boston (589,141)
Worcester (172,648)
Springfield (152,082)

LAND AREA
7,840 sq. mi.
(20,306 sq. km.)

MASSACHUSETTS

the bay state

The Massachuset—from whom the state's name originates—were just one of the Algonquian tribes that inhabited the area prior to English settlement in the early 1600s. One of the thirteen original colonies, Massachusetts was a center for protest in the years leading up the American Revolution.

The state also ushered in the Industrial Revolution in the U.S.—it developed water-powered textile and shoe factories in the 1800s. Stony and infertile terrain, largely unsuited to farming, made the state's residents look to many different industries for income. Summers are hot and humid, with average temperatures of 68°F to 72°F (20°C to 22°C), while winters are cold, with the heaviest snowfall in the western part of the state.

The southern coastal region, consisting of the peninsula of Cape Cod and the islands of Nantucket and Martha's Vineyard, has a thriving tourist industry thanks to its great natural beauty. Fishing and cranberry farming are also practiced here. Boston, the state's capital, first developed as a seaport and center of intellectual and cultural life in early America. Today, Boston remains the center of finance, commerce, and culture in New England as well as a popular tourist destination.

VERMONT

NEW YORK

Connecticut River

TACONIC RANGE

• Pittsfield
• Hancock Village

• Tanglewood

MASSAC

BERKSHIRE HILLS

Connecticut River

Quabbin
Reservoir

Springfield •

CONNECTICUT

A HARVEST FEAST
A year after 102 Pilgrims landed at Plymouth in 1620, only 51 were still alive. Disease had taken a heavy toll during the winter of 1621. With 90 Wampanoag, the Pilgrims gratefully celebrated their harvest with a three-day festival. It was this harvest celebration that became the legend of the first Thanksgiving.

THE BATTLE OF BUNKER HILL
The Battle of Bunker Hill, the first major battle of the American Revolution, was fought in the Boston area. There, in June 1775, patriot forces roundly defeated the British. The Massachusetts colony had a long history of protest against British rule. It was the site of some of the most important boycotts and rebel actions, including the Boston Tea Party, and previous battles, including Lexington and Concord.

SHAKERS OF INNOVATION
In 1783, the Shakers, a religious sect devoted to pacifism and living a simple, productive life, established Hancock Village, which today showcases distinctive Shaker furniture and crafts. The Shakers were inventors, too. They invented many items used today, including the potato peeler.

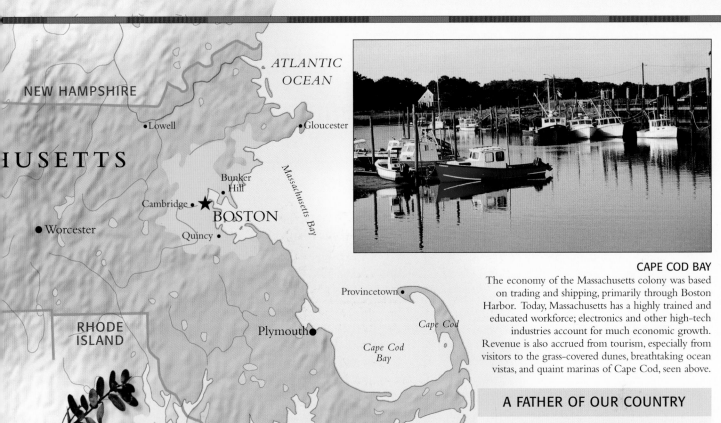

ATLANTIC OCEAN

NEW HAMPSHIRE

•Lowell

•Gloucester

...HUSETTS

Massachusetts Bay

Bunker Hill

Cambridge •★
BOSTON

•Worcester

Quincy •

Provincetown •

Cape Cod

Plymouth•

Cape Cod Bay

RHODE ISLAND

•New Bedford

Nantucket Sound

Martha's Vineyard

Nantucket
Nantucket

CAPE COD BAY

The economy of the Massachusetts colony was based on trading and shipping, primarily through Boston Harbor. Today, Massachusetts has a highly trained and educated workforce; electronics and other high-tech industries account for much economic growth. Revenue is also accrued from tourism, especially from visitors to the grass-covered dunes, breathtaking ocean vistas, and quaint marinas of Cape Cod, seen above.

A FATHER OF OUR COUNTRY

JOHN ADAMS

John Adams was one of the major figures of the Revolutionary era. He helped lead the Continental Congress to declare independence from Great Britain, later serving the new nation as an ambassador, vice president, and finally as the second U.S. president. Born in Braintree (now Quincy), Massachusetts, in 1735, Adams authored the state's constitution in 1780. Those who framed the U.S. Constitution were influenced by this document. As president, Adams's diplomacy skills averted a potentially disastrous war with France.

At 5'4" tall, John Adams was the shortest U.S. president.

THE "BERRY" BEST

The state's rocky and often mountainous terrain is best suited to the growth of specialty crops and dairy farming. Half of the nation's cranberry crop is grown on Cape Cod and its surrounding counties. The cultivation of flowers, plants, and shrubs for professional and amateur landscapers contributes to the state's farming production, as do crops such as pumpkins and butternut squash.

DID YOU KNOW?

Massachusetts's state fruit, the cranberry, is one of only three widely cultivated fruits native to North America. The other two fruits are the blueberry and the Concord grape, both of which are also grown in Massachusetts.

ON YOUR MARK, GET SET...

More than 5,000 runners compete every year in the Boston Marathon, the oldest foot race in the nation, dating from 1897. But Massachusetts also has more—history buffs, beach lovers, theater-goers, and outdoor enthusiasts alike all have something to choose from. There are important historic sites, including Plimoth Plantation, a re-creation of the first Pilgrim settlement, as well as the sun and surf of Cape Cod and Nantucket.

BEAUTIFUL BERKSHIRES

The Berkshire Mountains in western Massachusetts are home to many summertime cultural events. They include classical and jazz concerts at Tanglewood, dance at Jacob's Pillow, and a Shakespeare festival. Meanwhile, the state's Atlantic coast boasts rolling hills, natural harbors, beautiful beaches, and sand dunes. Massachusetts's bountiful streams and rivers powered the state's industrial development and influenced the state's economy and settlement patterns.

STATE BIRD
American Robin

STATE FLOWER
Mountain Laurel

STATE TREE
White Oak

CAPITAL
Hartford

POPULATION
3,405,565 (2000)

STATEHOOD
January 9, 1788
Rank: 5th

LARGEST CITIES
Bridgeport (139,529)
New Haven (123,626)
Hartford (121,578)

LAND AREA
4,845 sq. mi.
(12,549 sq. km.)

CONNECTICUT
the constitution state

Among the first people in the Connecticut region were numerous Algonquian tribes such as the Mohegan. The Algonquian had a large impact on the area—even Connecticut's name is a variation of an Algonquian word meaning "on the long tidal river." European exploration of the region began in 1614 when Dutchman Adriaen Block sailed up the Connecticut River. He claimed his surroundings as part of the Dutch colony of New Netherlands. Although the Dutch built a small fort where Hartford is today, British colonists from Massachusetts created the first permanent white settlements in the area, and eventually formed the Connecticut Colony in 1636.

Connecticut's rich history includes great contributions to the American Revolution, as well as events such as the trial surrounding the fate of the slave ship *Amistad* and the publication of Harriet Beecher Stowe's *Uncle Tom's Cabin*, which helped rally public support for the war against slavery.

Modern Connecticut is home to Yale University and a wide range of industries, including a growing cluster of biotechnology research companies. Residents and visitors enjoy the state's colorful leaves in autumn, as well as its coastal resorts and historical sites such as Mystic Seaport.

Litchfield
County

NEW YORK

Litchfield

Housatonic River

• Danbury

New Haven •

• Ridgefield

• Bridgeport

• Norwalk

Long Island Sound

• Stamford

DID YOU KNOW?
The Hartford Courant, established in 1764, is the U.S.'s oldest continuously published newspaper.

THE AMISTAD
In 1839, 53 Africans onboard the Spanish ship *Amistad* mutinied and tried to sail back to Africa. The ship ended up in Long Island Sound, off the coast of Connecticut. The governments of Cuba and Spain sued for the return of their "property," but the Connecticut courts held that the Africans were free men. Today, a replica of the *Amistad*, constructed at Mystic Seaport, sails around the world to remind people of the kidnapped Africans' plight.

IVY LEAGUE UNIVERSITY
New Haven is home to the country's third oldest institution of higher learning: Yale University. The Ivy League university opened in 1701 as the Collegiate School in the Killington, Connecticut, home of its first leader, Abraham Pierson. In 1716, the school moved to New Haven. Two years later, it was renamed in honor of Elihu Yale, who provided the school with gifts that included 417 books and a portrait of King George I.

MASSACHUSETTS

★ HARTFORD

CONNECTICUT

RHODE ISLAND

Connecticut River

● Norwich

● New London

Mystic

Mystic Seaport ●

MYSTICAL MYSTIC

One of the state's most popular tourist attractions is Mystic Seaport, a re-creation of a 19th century waterfront village and shipyard. Visitors to the port on the Mystic River can view the *Charles W. Morgan*, the world's last wooden whaling ship still afloat, as well as a 1921 fishing schooner and other ships of the period. They can also watch craftsman build ships and make soap and candles.

PATRIOT WEEKEND

On April 27, 1777, British troops began to advance south from Danbury, Connecticut. When they reached the small town of Ridgefield, Patriots—colonists who wanted independence from Britain—led by General Benedict Arnold fought back. Many were left dead on both sides, and the Patriots were forced to retreat. After the battle, thousands gathered in Connecticut to protect it from future attacks. Today Ridgefield residents and military buffs re-create the battle every year.

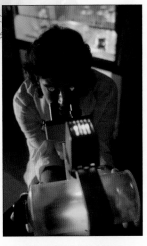

BIOTECH RESEARCH

Connecticut is the site of at least 12 percent of the nation's pharmaceutical research, which includes the profitable manufacture of new, powerful drugs to treat diseases.

FREEDOM WRITER

HARRIET BEECHER STOWE

Harriet Beecher Stowe's popular novel *Uncle Tom's Cabin* helped abolitionists deliver the message that slavery was cruel and immoral. Born in 1811 in Litchfield, she was one of 11 children highly influenced by their father, the Reverend Lyman Beecher. Stowe first formulated her strong feelings against slavery by listening to her father's sermons. Her writing skills were developed at the Hartford Female Seminary, a school run by her sister, Catharine.

Uncle Tom's Cabin sold more than 10,000 copies in its first week.

NEW ENGLAND AUTUMN

In the fall, Connecticut's Litchfield County provides travelers driving along its winding country roads with a burst of color as its tree leaves change for the season. Forestland makes up more than 60 percent of the state, with birch, elm, hickory, maple, and oak being among the most common trees.

FAIR STATE, FAIR WEATHER

Connecticut's Long Island Sound is busy with recreational boats throughout the year. The state's weather is mild—precipitation averages 47 inches (119 cm). Average temperatures range from 26°F (-3°C) in January to 71°F (22°C) in July, though it is generally colder and snowier in the northwest.

STATE FACTS

STATE BIRD
Rhode Island Red

STATE FLOWER
Violet

STATE TREE
Red Maple

CAPITAL
Providence

POPULATION
1,048,319 (2000)

STATEHOOD
May 29, 1790
Rank: 13th

LARGEST CITIES
Providence (173,618)
Warwick (85,808)
Cranston (79,269)

LAND AREA
1,045 sq. mi.
(2,707 sq. km.)

RHODE ISLAND

the ocean state

A few thousand Algonquian, including the Narragansett, lived in the region when European explorers first arrived. In 1511, Miguel de Cortereal of Portugal may have been the first to lead an expedition along the Rhode Island coastline. The origin of the state name is unclear, but some historians believe it was named by Italian explorer Giovanni da Verrazano, who believed that the land resembled the Mediterranean island of Rhodes. Other historians think it was named by Dutch sailor Adriaen Block, who called an island in Narragansett Bay "Roodt Eylandt" (Red Island) because of the red clay on its shore.

In 1636, a minister, Roger Williams, established the region's first permanent settlement by white people at Providence. Williams had left the Massachusetts colony seeking political and religious freedom. Two years later, other Massachusetts colonists left for similar reasons. They settled Pocasset on Aquidneck Island. Anne Hutchinson left Aquidneck and founded Portsmouth at Pocasset, while William Coddington and John Clarke established Newport. Another settlement, Warwick, was founded in 1643. Williams proposed that these settlements unite to protect themselves from other colonies. In 1663, they officially became Rhode Island and Providence Plantations.

Rhode Islanders took part in one of the most famous colonial acts of defiance, the burning of the British ship *Gaspee,* but no other American Revolution battles took place on Rhode Island soil. On May 29, 1790, Rhode Island became the last of the original 13 colonies to approve the U.S. Constitution. Today, tourists flock to the state's many islands, in particular Block Island, to enjoy sailing and beaches. On land, visitors can amuse themselves by visiting unique landmarks to Mr. Potato Head and the Rhode Island Red, the chicken that is the state's official bird.

CONNECTICUT

Westerly

BURNING OF GASPEE

The British schooner *Gaspee* was burned on June 10, 1772 at present-day Gaspee Point in Narragansett Bay. Many Rhode Islanders smuggled goods to avoid paying taxes, and their activities were frustrated by the ship's presence. On June 9, the ship sailed near Providence while chasing a suspected smuggler. Prominent Providence men boarded *Gaspee,* wounded the commander, took hold of the crew, and set fire to the ship. The event marked one of the most famous acts of colonial defiance before the American Revolution began.

RHODE ISLAND RED

It may seem odd that in 1954 a chicken was named Rhode Island's state bird, but Rhode Islanders are proud of the Rhode Island Red. Developed in the 1850s on a farm in Little Compton, it was considered the best breed in the U.S. at that time. It was a source of both good meat and eggs. Today, the Red Rock Chicken, a cross between the Rhode Island Red and another chicken, is the most popular variety for meat and eggs.

MASSACHUSETTS

• Woonsocket

DID YOU KNOW?
Rhode Island is the smallest state. Slightly more than 547 Rhode Island-sized states could fit inside Alaska.

Pawtucket •

PROVIDENCE ★

Cranston •

MASSACHUSETTS

Warwick •

Tiverton •

RHODE ISLAND

Narragansett Bay

Kingston •

Newport •

Little Compton •

Rhode Island Sound

Block Island

NEWPORT JAZZ FESTIVAL
The Newport Jazz Festival has been a summer tradition since July 1954, and is the world's oldest continually held jazz festival. The festival showcases jazz musicians from around the world. Some famous performers have been Billie Holiday, Louis Armstrong, Dave Brubeck, and even comedian Bill Cosby's band, Cos of Good Music.

GROWN IN RHODE ISLAND
Rhode Island isn't known for its potatoes, but it has made an industry with a potato head. Since 1952 Pawtucket-based toy company Hasbro has been manufacturing Mr. Potato Head. Mr. Potato Head was the first toy ever to be advertised on television.

THE BREAKERS, NEWPORT BEACH
Newport's biggest mansion is Rhode Island's most popular tourist attraction. The Breakers, a summer home built by Cornelius Vanderbilt II in the 1890s, has 70 rooms. During the late-nineteenth century, Newport was a summer playground for many of the nation's wealthiest people, who tried to outdo each other by building ever-larger houses.

CIVIL WAR SONGWRITER

JULIA WARD HOWE

In 1861, Julia Ward Howe wrote "The Battle Hymn of the Republic," an anthem set to the tune of the then-popular song "John Brown's Body." She received $4 for its publication in *The Atlantic Monthly* but received national attention when it became the Union's anthem during the Civil War. Howe, who had dedicated herself to antislavery causes before the war, advocated for women's right to vote, as well as other causes after the war ended.

Julia Ward Howe lived to be 91 years old

BLOCK ISLAND
Block Island is a favorite tourist getaway and includes the Mohegan Bluffs, which tower above sea level and stretch for almost 3 miles (5 km) along the island's southern shoreline. Block Island's harbor is the final stop for ferry riders from Connecticut, Long Island, and mainland Rhode Island. More than 300 ponds as well as rolling grassy hills, beaches, coves, and the Southeast Lighthouse mark the island. The lighthouse features the most powerful electric light on the eastern coast.

NEW YORK
the empire state

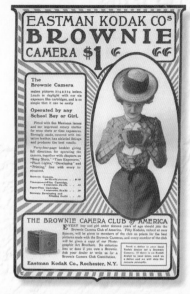

THE KODAK BROWNIE
In 1888, George Eastman invented the Brownie, a reasonably priced, "point and shoot" camera. Today the Eastman Kodak Company remains headquartered in Rochester.

Around 1570, the Cayuga, Mohawk, Oneida, Onondaga, and Seneca, all of whom lived in the central part of the present-day state, joined to form the Iroquois Confederacy. This powerful American Indian alliance provided support to its British allies as they tried to gain control of North America from other European nations. The British originally gained control of the region by seizing the Dutch colony New Netherlands in 1664. The colony was renamed New York, after the Duke of York, the British king's brother, and was one of the thirteen original colonies.

Between 1817 and 1825, the Erie Canal was built—it connected the port of New York City to the Great Lakes. This transportation revolution made the state into a national leader in trade and manufacturing.

The Empire State lives up to its name as a center of international shipping and finance, a leading manufacturer of goods including printed material and electronic equipment, and a leading producer of farm goods such as apples, grapes, and potatoes. This state offers something for everyone with regions of breath-taking natural beauty for outdoor recreation as well as the cultural and educational attractions of one of the world's greatest cities, New York City.

CLINTON'S DITCH
Governor DeWitt Clinton's idea for a canal across New York state was mockingly called "Clinton's Ditch." The Erie Canal eventually ran from the city of Buffalo on Lake Erie to Albany on the Hudson River, thereby linking the settled eastern seaboard with the Midwest. The rise of New York City as the nation's leading metropolitan center can be traced to the canal.

BUY! SELL!
The New York Stock Exchange, the world's largest market for trading securities, was founded in 1792 by 24 New York City merchants and stockbrokers. Today, more than 3,000 companies in the U.S. and abroad are listed and their stocks are traded on floor of the NYSE.

THE BIG APPLE

Upstate New York and eastern Long Island are home to thriving agricultural economies. Dairy farms abound in the state's river valleys, and the state is among the nation's top producers of maple syrup and grapes. Due to the state's abundant grape crop, vineyards that produce fine wines are plentiful. Meanwhile, each year New York and Michigan vie for second place (after Washington state) in the national production of apples. New York's apple crop has generated as much as $10.7 billion annually.

MIGHTY FALLS

Located on the river of the same name along the border between western New York and Ontario, Canada, the water power of Niagara Falls has long been harnessed for human use; today two major hydroelectric power plants operate here. The beauty of the site has made it a popular tourist destination.

MEMORIAL LIGHTS

On September 11, 2001, more than 3,000 people died in terrorist attacks that targeted New York City and Washington, D.C. The massive rescue and recovery operation, begun immediately after two airliners crashed into the World Trade Center towers, has become a symbol of courage and dedication in the face of tragedy. On the six-month anniversary of the event, two great columns of light illuminated the night sky, memorializing the towers and all who died in them.

PIONEERING SUFFRAGETTE

SUSAN B. ANTHONY

Susan Brownell Anthony, teacher, reformer, and leader in the struggle for the vote and equal rights for American women, lived most of her life in upstate New York, primarily in Rochester. Anthony's work in the temperance and abolition movements led her to the women's rights movement of the 1850s. Although Anthony died in 1906, her body of work and the organizations she helped to found played a central role in the 1920 passage of the Nineteenth Amendment, which granted women the right to vote.

Anthony was arrested for voting in the 1872 presidential election.

DID YOU KNOW?

The first bank robbery in the U.S. took place in 1831, at the City Bank in New York City.

STATE BIRD
Eastern Goldfinch

STATE FLOWER
Purple Violet

STATE TREE
Red Oak

CAPITAL
Trenton

POPULATION
8,414,350 (2000)

STATEHOOD
December 18, 1787
Rank: 3rd

LARGEST CITIES
Newark (273,546)
Jersey City (240,055)
Paterson (149,222)

LAND AREA
7,417 sq. mi.
(19,210 sq. km.)

NEW JERSEY

the garden state

Giovanni da Verrazano was the first European to explore New Jersey's coast in 1524. It was Henry Hudson's 1609 explorations, however, and especially the accounts of Dutch explorer Cornelius Mey's 1614 expedition, that encouraged the Netherlands to found the region's first settlement by white people in Pavonia (part of present-day Jersey City). Before the Dutch arrived in the 1630s, as many as 8,000 American Indians, mostly Leni-Lenape, whom the Europeans called the Delaware, lived there.

The British won control of New Jersey in 1664. The colony's location between New York City and Philadelphia made it a frequent battleground during the American Revolution. Almost 100 battles were fought in New Jersey, including the 1776 Battle of Trenton, an important victory for the Revolutionary forces.

In the early 1900s, New Jersey became a huge center of industry and invention. Thomas Alva Edison opened a lab in Menlo Park, which became the site of many of his most famous inventions. Around the same time, the Johnson brothers opened Johnson & Johnson, now an international pharmaceutical company with headquarters in New Brunswick. Today, state income also gets a big boost from the cultivation of plants and produce.

One of New Jersey's most visited features is its 130-mile (209 km) shore along the Atlantic. The shore is lined with long, narrow islands called barrier islands that were formed over thousands of years by rivers washing sand and silt into the ocean.

DID YOU KNOW?
The first drive-in movie theater opened on June 6, 1933 in Camden, New Jersey. Movie lovers came in droves to watch films on the 40 by 50 foot (12 by 15 m) outdoor screen.

COLONISTS' SNEAK ATTACK
The victory of colonial troops at the American Revolution Battle of Trenton in 1776 was due in part to a sneak attack. General George Washington led his men across the icy Delaware River on Christmas Day and caught the Hessian forces—German soldiers serving in the British army—by surprise. Many battles of the American Revolution were fought in New Jersey: it became known as the "cockpit of the revolution."

WIZARD OF MENLO PARK
Inventor Thomas Edison opened a laboratory in Menlo Park in 1876. During the next 10 years, he improved upon the telephone and invented the first electric lightbulb, movie projector, and camera. Of Edison's 1,093 inventions, 400 were developed in his Menlo Park lab.

Map labels:
PENNSYLVANIA
Delaware Water Ga.
Delaware River
Phillipsburg
NEW
TRENTON ★
PENNSYLVANIA
Philadelphia
Camden
Cherry Hill
Lindenwold
Pitman
DELAWARE
Delaware River
Pennsville
Vineland
Bridgeton
Millville
Port Norris
Delaware Bay
North Wildwood
Cape Ma

FOR THEIR AMUSEMENT

The Jersey Shore's 130-mile (209 km) coastline contains everything from the casinos of Atlantic City to historic Cape May with its brightly colored Victorian houses as well as pristine beaches. The town of Wildwood's boardwalk (pictured above) features the tallest Ferris wheel in the East and one of only four suspended looping roller coasters in the world. The city of Wildwood is located on Wildwood's Five Mile Island.

JOHNSON & JOHNSON

Johnson & Johnson opened its headquarters in New Brunswick in 1885. Today, it is the world's largest pharmaceutical corporation with 197 companies that sell surgical supplies, medicine, and their most famous product, Band-Aid adhesive bandages, which were invented by an employee in 1921.

PRODUCE AND PLANTS

Less than one percent of the state's population works on farms, but New Jersey's 8,700 farms provide food for millions of people. The state ranks among the top in production of blueberries, cranberries, apples, lettuce, tomatoes, and peaches. In the northeast, nurseries and greenhouses grow flowers and shrubs, most of which are sold in New York City flower shops. After greenhouse products and nursery plants, the state's biggest farm product is milk. The fertile soils of the northwestern part of the state make it ideal for dairy farms.

LARGEST EASTERN RECREATION SITE

The Delaware Water Gap National Recreation Area is a 70,000-acre (112,651 hectare) park that stretches through New Jersey and Pennsylvania. It consists of a canyon carved by the waters of the Delaware River. Each year three million visitors come to the park—the largest recreation area in the East—to climb Mount Tammany, explore the late-nineteenth-century re-created community of Millbrook Village, walk along the park's 25 miles (40 km) of the Appalachian Trail, or simply relax in its picnic areas or beaches.

"OL' BLUE EYES"

FRANK SINATRA

Hoboken-born Francis Albert Sinatra worked at a local newspaper before launching a singing career. In the late 1930s and early 1940s, he sang with Henry James and Tommy Dorsey's big bands. Sinatra continued recording and entertaining live audiences on his own, even after his retirement in 1971. His biggest hits, including "My Way" and "New York New York," have become classics. Sinatra also made 58 films and won an academy award in 1953 for his role in *From Here to Eternity*.

Sinatra's career spanned 70 years.

STATE FLOWER
Mountain Laurel

STATE TREE
Hemlock

CAPITAL
Harrisburg

POPULATION
12,281,054 (2000)

STATEHOOD
December 12, 1787
Rank: 2nd

LARGEST CITIES
Philadelphia (1,517,550)
Pittsburgh (334,563)
Allentown (106,632)

LAND AREA
44,817 sq. mi.
(116,076 sq. km.)

PENNSYLVANIA
the keystone state

In 1681 King Charles II of England gave his advisor William Penn, a Quaker, control of a piece of North American land to honor a debt. Penn named the colony for his father—*Pennsylvania* means "Penn's woods." Penn, who never lived in Pennsylvania, told the colony's government to deal honorably with the Leni-Lenape, Shawnee, and other American Indians, which resulted in their peaceful coexistence with white settlers for more than seven decades.

Originally established as a haven for Quakers and other religious dissenters, white settlements sprang up rapidly. Since the first English Quakers' arrival, Pennsylvania's culture has been shaped by waves of immigrants: the Germans, or Pennsylvania "Dutch," who settled in the southeast included the Amish who dress distinctively and reject modernity to this day.

Founded in the spirit of freedom and brotherly love, the city of Philadelphia hosted some of the major political events of the Revolutionary period, including the signing of the Declaration of Independence.

The state has always had a diversified economy because of its wealth of natural resources, including navigable waterways, abundant fossil fuel deposits, timber, and fertile farmland.

Philadelphia and Pittsburgh constitute the state's two major metropolitan centers, which combined are home to more than half the state's total population. High humidity in the summer and heavy snowfall in the winter represent the extremes of the region's climate— yet another example of the natural advantages that have made Pennsylvania one of the nation's most prosperous states.

DID YOU KNOW?

Pennsylvania is actually a commonwealth, not a state. The word comes from an Old English word meaning "the common good."

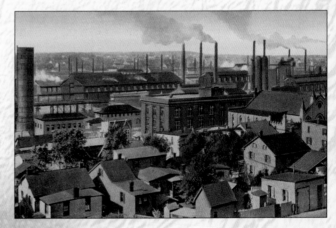

THE CIVIL WAR
Slavery was outlawed in Pennsylvania in 1780, and the state became an abolitionist stronghold in the years leading up to the Civil War. The state fought on the side of the Union during this bloody conflict. The invasion of Confederate forces into the North was stopped at the Battle of Gettysburg, which raged from July 1 to July 3, 1863. This decisive Union victory resulted in more than 43,000 casualties, making it one of the deadliest battles of the war.

GETTING THE GOODS
Huge "steel towns" such as Bethlehem flourished in the 1800s, when the state's abundant coal, iron ore, and oil deposits made it a national leader in the production of iron and steel. Pennsylvania's mining, processing, and manufacturing first became concentrated within the state boundaries by Andrew Carnegie. While industry and manufacturing, centered in Pittsburgh and Philadelphia, still contribute to the livelihood of the state's residents, Pennsylvania also has a healthy agricultural economy, which includes dairy farms, apple orchards, and wheat fields.

PENNSYLVANIA

NEW YORK

Allegheny Plateau

Delaware River

Susquehanna River

Appalachian Mountains

Allegheny Mountains

Blue Ridge Mountains

NEW JERSEY

Allentown •Bethlehem

Lebanon

★ HARRISBURG

Philadelphia•

• Gettysburg

DE

MARYLAND

A LITTLE KISS

The Hershey Foods Corporation was founded in Pennsylvania in 1894 and has made the state the nation's leader in chocolate production. The famous Hershey's Kiss was first introduced in 1907. Today, this state's other products include industrial machinery as well as high-tech products, such as computer chips and cell phones.

PUNXSUTAWNEY PHIL

This Pennsylvania resident forecasts the future. If he doesn't see his shadow on February 2, spring is supposedly on its way. Groundhog Day is a reminder of the importance of weather to the livelihood of America's farmers, and of early German immigrants who brought the groundhog tradition to this country.

UNBROKEN TRADITION

In the early 1700s German immigrants, many seeking to escape persecution for their religious beliefs, established farms in southeastern Pennsylvania. The Amish, a Christian sect that still dresses and lives today much as it did three hundred years ago, were among these early immigrants. The Amish reject telephones, cars, televisions, and other modern technology due to their religious beliefs.

APPALACHIAN BEAUTY

Pennsylvania's climate is rainy in springtime, humid and warm in summer, and cold and snowy in winter. Statewide variation is caused by land elevation. The lowlands around Philadelphia, the state's southeast, and the west-central valleys all have a more temperate climate with a longer growing season. The Blue Ridge and Allegheny Mountains (at right) to the south and the Allegheny Plateau to the north average about 69°F (21°C) in summer and 25°F (-4°C) in winter, with heavy snows.

MOTHER OF ENVIRONMENTALISM

RACHEL CARSON

Born in Springdale, Pennsylvania, Rachel Carson trained as a biologist, taught college, and worked for the U.S. Fish and Wildlife Service. Carson wrote widely on the natural world; her scientific expertise, combined with her polished and lyrical writing style, brought her a wide readership, well beyond her fellow scientists. Her 1962 book *Silent Spring* focused on the dangers of pollution and helped inspire the modern environmental movement, which arose shortly thereafter.

Silent Spring *was very controversial at the time of its publication.*

DECEMBER 7, 1787

DELAWARE
the first state

Two tribes of Algonquian Indians—the Leni-Lenape and the Nanticoke—lived in the region when British explorer Henry Hudson sailed into Delaware Bay in 1609. Captain Samuel Argall, from Britain's Virginia colony, sailed into the bay the following year, naming it for the colony's governor, Lord Del La Warr. It was the Dutch, however, who established the area's first European settlement in 1631, a fort that stood at what is now the city of Lewes. Within a year, battles with American Indians led to the fort's destruction in a fire.

Swedes established the area's first permanent colony, New Sweden, in 1638. Their first settlement was Fort Christina. By the mid-1700s, few American Indians remained, and the Dutch had taken control of the colony from Sweden. The region later fell into British hands in 1664. When Delaware settlers complained about being grouped with Pennsylvanians, they were allowed to set up their own legislature. Two years after the beginning of the American Revolution, the area was named Delaware State.

Delaware has long benefited financially from the manufacturing industry, beginning with the DuPont gunpowder mills that prospered during the American Revolution, through today's profitable chemical and banking industries. Its most popular vacation spot is Rehoboth Beach. Thanks to the Delaware Memorial Bridge, residents are linked to New Jersey; to the west, Washington, D.C. is an easy drive.

PENNSYLVANIA

Wilmington
Fort Christina
Delaware River
Newark
Delaware Memorial Bridge
Pea Patch Island

NEW JERSEY

Middletown

MARYLAND

Smyrna

DOVER ★

Camden

Murderkill River

Guilford

DELAW

DID YOU KNOW?

Many Delaware rivers include *kill* in their names, as that was the old Dutch word for river. The Dutch named Murderkill River as "Mother River," but since it was spelled as "Murther," the English mistook it for "Murder."

Seaford

Laurel

MARYLAND

PEA PATCH ISLAND/FORT DELAWARE

Pea Patch Island in the Delaware River was formed in the late 1700s when a ship carrying peas hit a sandbar. Peas were dumped into the sea and grew into plants that collected enough sand to create an island. During the War of 1812, Fort Delaware was built on the island to guard Philadelphia from a British attack. The fort was rebuilt in the 1850s and served as a prison during the Civil War. At one point, it held more than 12,000 prisoners, many of whom suffered from malnutrition or died of smallpox and other diseases. Today, the fort is a state park with a large population of wading birds, including herons and egrets.

FORT CHRISTINA

Delaware's first permanent settlement was Fort Christina, established by Swedish colonists in late March 1638. Among the settlers was Delaware's first African, an indentured servant from the Caribbean named Antonious. In 1655, conflict between Sweden and the Netherlands over territory led to the destruction of the New Sweden colony. Some Swedes stayed in Delaware under Dutch rule.

VARIED WILDLIFE

Snow geese migrate through Delaware in early fall, stoppng in the state's wetlands. Other birds, such as ruby-throated hummingbirds, are common to the state. Otters and foxes live in forest and field areas, while snapping turtles and muskrats are found in marshes and swamps. Commercial and recreational fishers enjoy the state's coastal waters, which are full of clams, crabs, and striped bass.

A LIFESAVING VISIONARY

DR. HENRY J. HEIMLICH

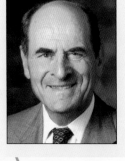

Wilmington-born Dr. Henry J. Heimlich's first medical breakthrough came in 1945, when he found a treatment for trachoma, an infection that causes blindness. His treatment saved the sight of hundreds of people. In the 1950s, he developed a technique to replace the esophagus. This operation was the world's first full organ transplant. In 1964, he introduced a valve that drains blood and air from chest injuries. Today, more than 250,000 of these valves are used each year.

Heimlich's most famous innovation, the Heimlich Maneuver, was introduced in 1974 to save choking victims.

DELAWARE MEMORIAL BRIDGE

The 2,150-foot- (655-m-) long Delaware Memorial Bridge is the world's longest twin-span bridge. Each day more than 100,000 people cross the bridge, which serves as a memorial to Delaware and New Jersey members of the armed forces who died in World War II, the Korean War, and Vietnam.

E • Lewes

Rehoboth Beach •

• Selbyville

ATLANTIC OCEAN

Delaware Bay

HISTORIC BEACH

Rehoboth Beach, on the state's southeastern coast has been popular with summer visitors for more than 100 years. The beach is lined by one of the last remaining wooden boardwalks on the Atlantic. The first U.S. beauty contest was held at Rehoboth in 1880. Among the three judges voting on "Miss United States" was inventor Thomas Edison. Today the one-square-mile (three-sq-km) resort town receives six million visitors each year, including many Washington, D.C., residents who have summer homes there.

DUPONT LABORATORIES

DuPont, one of the world's largest chemical companies, is Delaware's largest employer. It began as an explosives manufacturer and has since created materials such as Lycra and Kevlar. In 1999, DuPont bought the country's largest seed producer and entered the growing field of agricultural engineering. Other chemical and pharmaceutical companies have relocated to Delaware, in part because of the many skilled chemical employees residing there.

MARYLAND
the old line state

• Cumberland

WEST VIRGINIA

European explorers visiting the Maryland region in the late 1500s encountered both Algonquian and Susquehannock peoples. The first Europeans to visit were the Spanish, in 1572. In 1608, Captain John Smith sailed north from the Virginia colony to the Chesapeake Bay. His description of the area eventually led King Charles I of England to grant the region to George Calvert, the first Lord Baltimore, in 1632. The region was named Maryland in honor of the king's wife, Queen Henrietta Maria.

Settlers were drawn to Maryland after it became famous among the colonies as a place where religious freedom was permitted. Maryland troops fought fiercely throughout the American Revolution, and also entered the fray during the War of 1812 and the Civil War, when they fought to preserve the Union. The state's nickname comes from its "heroic troops in a line," which were praised by George Washington.

As a result of its history, present-day Maryland has many historical tourist attractions, including Baltimore's Inner Harbor and the U.S. Naval Academy. Over the years, Maryland's Chesapeake Bay has both defined and been essential to the state's economy and lifestyle. The bay itself is home to the famous Thomas Point Lighthouse, as well as many fish and shellfish, including the blue crab. The waters are so important that the state even named the skipjack its state boat.

BLUE CRAB
This crustacean, or shellfish, lives all along the North Atlantic coast, but is especially prevalent in the Chesapeake Bay and its tributaries. Prized for its tasty flesh, nearly 50 percent of the nation's blue crab harvest comes from the Chesapeake Bay. While commonly called the blue crab, for its blue-gray shell, its Latin name, *Callinectes sapidus*, means "beautiful swimmer that is savory."

CHESAPEAKE BAY BRIDGE
The Chesapeake Bay Bridge connects Kent Island's Eastern Shore with the Western Shore near Annapolis, which are divided by the Chesapeake Bay. Before the bridge opened in 1952, travelers had to get to the Eastern Shore by ferry or travel halfway around the bay by vehicle. Fishing and crabbing in the bay brings in millions of dollars each year and more blue crabs than any other state.

U.S. NAVAL ACADEMY
Since it was founded in 1845, the U.S. Naval Academy at Annapolis has trained more than 60,000 naval officers. The school's location provides it with a large port where the Severn River meets the Chesapeake Bay. Students spend four years at the school, getting an education and learning to sail. Their summers are often spent on naval missions. Graduates include President James Earl (Jimmy) Carter.

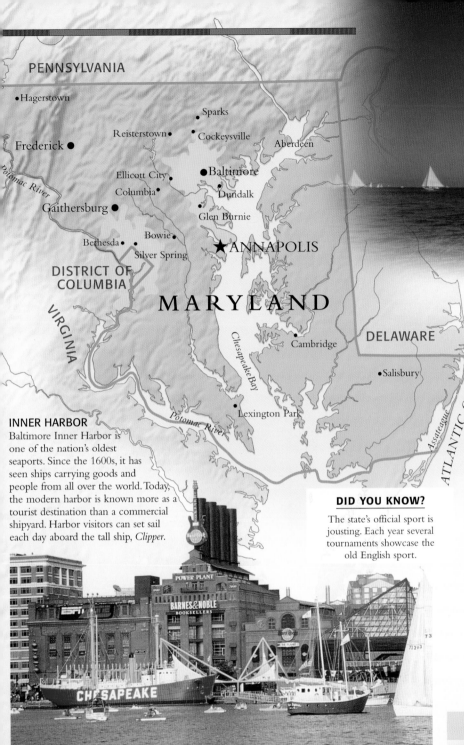

PENNSYLVANIA

Hagerstown

Sparks
Reisterstown • • Cockeysville
Frederick •
Aberdeen

Ellicott City •
Columbia • • Baltimore
Gaithersburg • • Dundalk
• Glen Burnie
Bethesda • Bowie •
Silver Spring •

DISTRICT OF
COLUMBIA

★ ANNAPOLIS

M A R Y L A N D

VIRGINIA

Potomac River

Chesapeake Bay

• Cambridge

DELAWARE

• Salisbury

• Lexington Park

Potomac River

Assateague

ATLANTIC OCEAN

STATE BOAT

Maryland's state boat, the skipjack, is considered to be among the last working sailboats in the U.S. Skipjacks were first used on Maryland's Eastern Shore in the 1890s. In winter, fleets of fast-moving skipjacks were typically used to dredge oysters from the floor of the Chesapeake Bay. The boat is named after fish, including tuna and mackerel, that "skip," or leap in and out of the water.

INNER HARBOR

Baltimore Inner Harbor is one of the nation's oldest seaports. Since the 1600s, it has seen ships carrying goods and people from all over the world. Today, the modern harbor is known more as a tourist destination than a commercial shipyard. Harbor visitors can set sail each day aboard the tall ship, *Clipper*.

DID YOU KNOW?

The state's official sport is jousting. Each year several tournaments showcase the old English sport.

ASSATEAGUE PONIES

Wild ponies wander the marshes of Assateague Island, a thin strip of land between the Eastern Shore and the Atlantic Ocean that is owned by Maryland and Virginia. No people live on the island, which is designated a National Seashore. As a result, the ponies roam freely. The ponies are most likely descendants of horses that were hidden on the island in the 17th century by owners who didn't want to pay taxes on them.

THE SULTAN OF SWAT

Ruth, born into poverty, was a tireless supporter of children's charities.

GEORGE HERMAN RUTH, JR.

George Herman "Babe" Ruth, born in Baltimore, Maryland, was a formidable pitcher for the Boston Red Sox before being traded to the New York Yankees in 1919. There he became the Yankee's best hitter, leading them to their first pennant in 1921, and six more thereafter, as well as four World Championships. Ruth became known as the "Sultan of Swat" because of his incredible hitting style. He held the career home-run record until Hank Aaron broke it in 1974.

LARGEST U.S. SPICE COMPANY

McCormick and Company's factory in Sparks, Maryland, manufactures common spices such as pepper as well as exotic ones such as saffron. The company is the largest spice manufacturer in the country. Among their famous seasonings is "Old Bay," a spice blend considered to be the perfect compliment to Maryland blue crabs. Meanwhile, Maryland's agricultural products include tobacco, which is raised in the southern half of the state. Twice as much money is derived from livestock and livestock products, however, as from crops.

THE SOUTHEAST STATES

St. Augustine, Florida, established by the Spanish in 1565, was the first permanent settlement by Europeans in what is today the U.S. By 1700, however, Virginia was North America's largest colony. The invention of the cotton gin in 1793 made cotton an important cash crop and led to population booms in Alabama and Mississippi. Meanwhile, American Indians were forced off their lands. One infamous episode was when the Creek and Cherokee were forced off their lands and made to walk the "Trail of Tears."

Charleston, West Virginia, the state's capital and largest city, was first settled in 1787. It is rich in architectural treasures dating back to the colonial period.

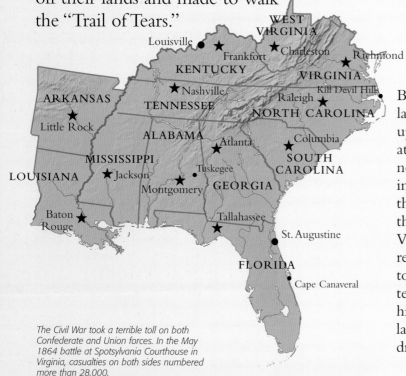

The Civil War took a terrible toll on both Confederate and Union forces. In the May 1864 battle at Spotsylvania Courthouse in Virginia, casualties on both sides numbered more than 28,000.

By the 1800s, slave labor became key to producing the large amount of cotton the Southern economy relied upon, and slavery became a contested issue. The attempt to balance the power of slave-holding and non-slave-holding states failed, leading to the Civil War in 1861. Most of the Southeastern states seceded from the Union at this time and created a new nation called the Confederate States of America. However, West Virginia joined the Union, and Kentucky attempted to remain neutral. The Southeast rebuilt after the war and today boasts a strong and diverse economy, including textile mills, citrus orchards, cutting-edge media, and high-tech businesses. The hospitable climate, beautiful landscape, and economic opportunities continue to draw many new residents and visitors to this region.

LANDSCAPE

White sand beaches, swamps, rugged mountains, fertile prairies, and more can be found in the Southeast. North and South Carolina have miles of Atlantic shoreline with sand dunes and barrier islands. The Florida peninsula is a beachcomber's paradise, with the islands of the Florida Keys extending into the Gulf of Mexico. The Mississippi River empties into the Gulf of Mexico, making Louisiana's Gulf Coast a complex ecosystem of swamps and bayous teeming with wildlife. Many mountain ranges are found inland, including the Great Smoky Mountains of Tennessee

KEY DATES

1565 The Spanish found St. Augustine, the first permanent European settlement in what will become the U.S.

1860 South Carolina is the first state to secede from the Union, sparking the Civil War. The war ends with the Confederacy's defeat in 1865.

1875 The Kentucky Derby is run for the first time at Churchill Downs in Louisville, Kentucky.

and the rugged Appalachian peaks of West Virginia. Some of the region's most fertile farmland, prairie land known as the Black Belt because of its rich soil, is found in south-central Alabama and Mississippi.

CLIMATE
The climate of the Southeast varies considerably based on elevation, proximity to the Atlantic and Gulf Coasts, and latitude, but inhabitants generally enjoy brief, mild winters with little snowfall and long, humid summers. The region's ample precipitation falls primarily as rain, as in Arkansas, with a yearly average of 43 inches (109 cm) of rain and only 6 inches (15 cm) of snow. Tropical storms and hurricanes are constant threats along the Atlantic and Gulf Coasts, particularly in the summer and fall. In August 2005, Hurricane Katrina struck the Gulf Coast, killing more than 1300 people and causing more than $130 billion in property damage, making it the U.S.'s costliest natural disaster.

The warm climate and fertile soil of the Southeast makes it the national leader in the production of cotton, rice, citrus fruits, and many other important agricultural products.

The National Hurricane Center, located in Florida, tracks hurricanes that originate in the Caribbean and Gulf of Mexico and frequently strike the Southeast's Atlantic and Gulf Coasts.

LIFESTYLE
Racing—whether horses or cars—is a big part of life in this region. Kentucky is horse country and home to the Kentucky Derby. Meanwhile, Charlotte, North Carolina, hosts NASCAR's Winston Select, which is only one of a multitude of auto races throughout the Southeast. The Southeast is the birthplace of blues, bluegrass, country music, and jazz and has produced many masters of American popular music, including Louis Armstrong and Aretha Franklin. Arkansas's yearly King Biscuit Blues Festival celebrates the musical dynamism of the region. New Orleans's Mardi Gras celebration highlights the amalgam of French, Spanish, African, and Anglo cultures that have created a distinctive way of life throughout the region. Historical sites abound in the Southwest; in Georgia, for example, there is a ceremonial mound dating back 1,000 years, as well as Andersonville Prison and other Civil War sites.

ECONOMY
Cotton was once the Southeast's most profitable crop, and it remains important today, along with citrus fruit in Florida, rice in Louisiana and Arkansas, and peaches in Georgia. Textiles are a major industry in the Carolinas and Alabama. Mining and glass-making are tops in West Virginia, and North Carolina is the nation's furniture-making center. Shrimp and oysters are important catches for commercial fisherman working off the Gulf Coast. Atlanta, New Orleans, and Miami are just a few of the Southeast's major urban centers for commerce and trade, with Atlanta being home to many major companies, including Coca-Cola. Tourism also plays a key role, with visitors sampling the culinary, musical, and athletic offerings of the Southeast's big cities.

Cotton is harvested into 500-pound bales. One bale of cotton can be used to make 215 pairs of jeans or 313,600 $100 bills. All U.S. paper money is 75 percent cotton.

1881 The Tuskegee Institute, later Tuskegee University, opens in Tuskegee, Alabama. This institution is dedicated to providing higher education for African-Americans.

1903 Wilbur and Orville Wright successfully fly the first motorized aircraft at Kill Devil Hills, near Kitty Hawk, North Carolina.

1963 Dr. Martin Luther King, Jr., leads a civil rights march from Selma to Montgomery, Alabama.

1969 Apollo II, launched from Cape Canaveral, Florida, reaches the Moon. Neil Armstrong becomes the first man to walk on the Moon's surface.

STATE BIRD
Cardinal

STATE FLOWER
Big Rhododendron

STATE TREE
Sugar Maple

CAPITAL
Charleston

POPULATION
1,808,344 (2000)

STATEHOOD
June 20, 1863
Rank: 35th

LARGEST CITIES
Charleston (53,421)
Huntington (51,475)
Parkersburg (33,099)

LAND AREA
24,078 sq. mi.
(62,362 sq. km.)

WEST VIRGINIA
the mountain state

West Virginia began as part of the Virginia Colony. That colony's land was granted to the Virginia Company of London—named for Elizabeth I, the Virgin Queen. Settlers moved into present-day West Virginia in the 1700s. Germans from Pennsylvania journeyed to the region to create one of the first settlements by white people, New Mecklenburg, in 1727. At the time, the Shawnee were among the region's American Indian population.

After the American Revolution, Virginia became a state. By the early 1800s, however, relations between western and eastern Virginia were strained, in part over the issue of slavery. Western Virginia was primarily made up of self-sufficient family farms, while eastern Virginia's economy was based on plantations that required slave labor. By August 1861, nearly five months after the Civil War began, western Virginians began the formal process of separating from the rest of the state, becoming a separate state two years later. The sympathies of the majority of the area's residents lay with the North, but Confederates—including Stonewall Jackson—also had power. As a result, more than 600 Civil War battles took place in West Virginia.

Today, West Virginia is known for its rugged landscapes. The state is also a national center for glassmaking. Its biggest industry, however, has long been coal mining. While citizens debate the modern—and now illegal—practice of mountaintop mining, tourists can tour a mine at Exhibition Coal Mine in New River Park.

GLASS PRODUCTION
West Virginia is one the nation's leaders in art glass production. Companies such as Marble King and Mid-Atlantic of West Virginia create marbles and decorative glass gems. The Blenko Glass Company in Milton provides stained glass for many famous churches, including the Washington National Cathedral in Washington, D.C.

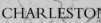

Parkersburg

OHIO

Ohio River

WES

Milton

Huntington

CHARLESTON

KENTUCKY

HARPERS FERRY
By the mid-1800s, the small town of Harpers Ferry was a major producer of weapons with numerous mills, gun factories, and huge stores of weapons and ammunition. Before the Civil War began, abolitionist John Brown tried to raid a U.S. arsenal. He wanted weapons so that he could invade the South and free slaves. The battle ended with Brown's defeat, and it was Robert E. Lee, later a Confederate general, who captured Brown and delivered him to his trial. Once the Civil War began, Harpers Ferry was an important strategic site. For most of the war's duration, Union soldiers held the town, though control changed hands many times. Its industrial plants were attacked repeatedly by Union and Confederate forces.

THE CITY OF CHARLESTON

Charleston, West Virginia's capital and largest city, lies along the banks of the Kanawha River. It's marked by a gold-domed capitol building that is 293 feet (89 m) tall—taller than the U.S. Capitol. Trees line much of the city, which is also the site of the governor's mansion and a memorial to civil rights reformer Booker T. Washington.

WILD WATER RIDE

West Virginia's mix of rocky terrain and rough waters make it an exciting spot for rafting. The Gauley River's rapids are internationally famous among white-water rafters. Although the river was once considered too wild for rafting, it now attracts around 60,000 rafters to West Virginia each year. White-water rafting is also popular on four of the state's other rivers.

DID YOU KNOW?

Golden Delicious apples were first grown on a farm in Clay County, West Virginia.

EXHIBITION COAL MINE

Former miners take visitors on an underground journey to see a turn-of-the-century mining operation at Exhibition Coal Mine. The mine in New River Park in the town of Beckley has 1,500 feet (457 m) of passages that were once operated by the Phillips family in the late 1800s. Coal camp buildings include a church, school, superintendent house, and a separate house for miners. The nearby Coal Museum provides a history of area mining in photographs and tools.

COAL MINING CONTROVERSY

For decades, environmentalists have battled West Virginia's mining industry on the issue of mountaintop mining. Mountaintop removal is a method that allows mining companies to cut off the tops of mountains to reach coal deposits below. The practice involves setting explosions to open the mountain and then dumping the mountaintop into nearby stream valleys. In May 2002, a federal judge put a stop to the practice by saying it was against federal environmental laws.

CONFEDERATE LEADER

THOMAS "STONEWALL" JACKSON

Jackson was born in Clarksburg, West Virginia, and attended West Point. When the Civil War broke out, he was made a colonel in the Confederate army and ordered to command at Harpers Ferry. Fighting under General Robert E. Lee, Jackson led his troops to many victories and became a lieutenant general. He was accidentally shot by his own men during the Confederate victory at Chancellorsville, in 1863.

Jackson earned his nickname at the Battle of Bull Run by standing, in the words of one general, "like a stone wall" against the North.

Map labels: Wheeling, PENNSYLVANIA, MD, Clarksburg, Harpers Ferry, APPALACHIAN MOUNTAINS, ALLEGHENY MOUNTAINS, IRGINIA, VIRGINIA, kley

VIRGINIA
old dominion state

A TEMPERATE CLIMATE
Virginia's climate is mild, and precipitation light—an average of 40 inches (102 cm) a year. In January, temperatures range between 32°F and 41°F (0°C and 5°C). July temperatures warm to an average of 68°F (20°C) in the mountains and about 78°F (26°C) elsewhere.

In 1584, Queen Elizabeth I of England permitted explorer Sir Walter Raleigh to establish colonies in North America. When the colonists first arrived in the region, tribes of Iroquois and Algonquian Native Americans lived there. The Algonquian tribes included the coastal-dwelling Powhatan. The early English expeditions failed, mainly because the settlers did not have the necessary supplies. In May 1607, English colonists led by Captain John Smith set up Virginia's first permanent English settlement in Jamestown.

By 1700, Virginia was the largest North American colony. Most Virginians were loyal to England but were frustrated by the taxes King George III imposed. Virginia leaders, including George Washington, protested. After the American Revolution and the passing of the Constitution, Washington's success made him a clear choice for the first U.S. president.

Tourists visit Virginia today to view Washington's beloved home, Mount Vernon, as well as Arlington National Cemetery. Some tourists are even able to tour part of the Pentagon, the headquarters of the nation's Department of Defense. Colonial life, including tobacco planting, is on display at Colonial Williamsburg. The state's scenery varies from mountains to tree-filled country roads and the Tidewater area's Great Dismal Swamp.

ARLINGTON NATIONAL CEMETERY
Arlington National Cemetery lies on land originally owned by George Washington's grandson, George Washington Parke Custis. Custis's daughter married soldier Robert E. Lee, and when Lee became a Confederate general, the Union Army took over the land for use as a cemetery. Now, Arlington is the country's largest national cemetery. Among its many military-related memorials is the Tomb of the Unknowns.

JAMESTOWN SETTLEMENT
British colonists, led by Captain John Smith, founded Jamestown, North America's first English settlement, in 1607. Many settlers died from lack of food, and there was also conflict with local American Indians. In 1612, colonist John Rolfe began to raise and cure tobacco, which provided the colony with income. The 1614 marriage between Rolfe and Pocahontas, of the Powhatan tribe, helped create a peace that lasted for about eight years.

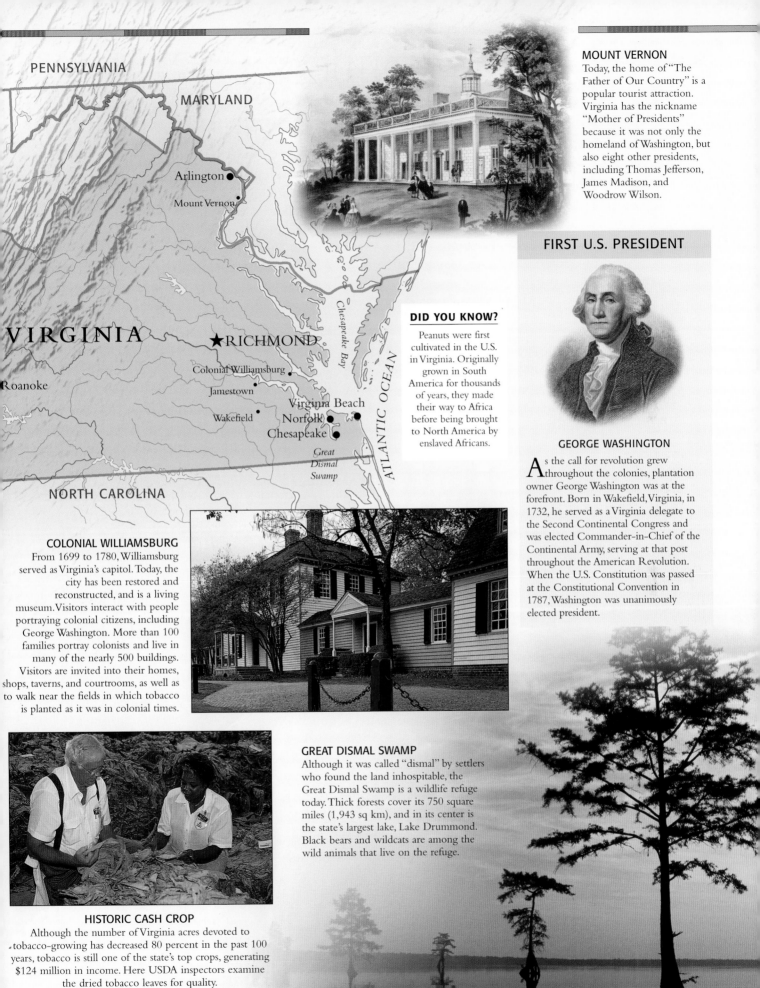

PENNSYLVANIA

MARYLAND

MOUNT VERNON
Today, the home of "The Father of Our Country" is a popular tourist attraction. Virginia has the nickname "Mother of Presidents" because it was not only the homeland of Washington, but also eight other presidents, including Thomas Jefferson, James Madison, and Woodrow Wilson.

Arlington ●

Mount Vernon ●

FIRST U.S. PRESIDENT

V I R G I N I A

★RICHMOND

Colonial Williamsburg ●

Jamestown ●

Roanoke

Wakefield ●

Virginia Beach
Norfolk ●
Chesapeake ●

Chesapeake Bay

ATLANTIC OCEAN

Great Dismal Swamp

NORTH CAROLINA

DID YOU KNOW?
Peanuts were first cultivated in the U.S. in Virginia. Originally grown in South America for thousands of years, they made their way to Africa before being brought to North America by enslaved Africans.

GEORGE WASHINGTON
As the call for revolution grew throughout the colonies, plantation owner George Washington was at the forefront. Born in Wakefield, Virginia, in 1732, he served as a Virginia delegate to the Second Continental Congress and was elected Commander-in-Chief of the Continental Army, serving at that post throughout the American Revolution. When the U.S. Constitution was passed at the Constitutional Convention in 1787, Washington was unanimously elected president.

COLONIAL WILLIAMSBURG
From 1699 to 1780, Williamsburg served as Virginia's capitol. Today, the city has been restored and reconstructed, and is a living museum. Visitors interact with people portraying colonial citizens, including George Washington. More than 100 families portray colonists and live in many of the nearly 500 buildings. Visitors are invited into their homes, shops, taverns, and courtrooms, as well as to walk near the fields in which tobacco is planted as it was in colonial times.

GREAT DISMAL SWAMP
Although it was called "dismal" by settlers who found the land inhospitable, the Great Dismal Swamp is a wildlife refuge today. Thick forests cover its 750 square miles (1,943 sq km), and in its center is the state's largest lake, Lake Drummond. Black bears and wildcats are among the wild animals that live on the refuge.

HISTORIC CASH CROP
Although the number of Virginia acres devoted to tobacco-growing has decreased 80 percent in the past 100 years, tobacco is still one of the state's top crops, generating $124 million in income. Here USDA inspectors examine the dried tobacco leaves for quality.

KENTUCKY
the bluegrass state

STATE BIRD
Cardinal

STATE FLOWER
Goldenrod

STATE TREE
Tulip Poplar

CAPITAL
Frankfort

POPULATION
4,041,769 (2000)

STATEHOOD
June 1, 1792
Rank: 15th

LARGEST CITIES
Lexington-Fayette
(260,512)
Louisville (256,231)
Owensboro (54,067)

LAND AREA
39,728 sq. mi.
(102,896 sq. km.)

In the late 1600s to early 1700s, English and French explorers visited the region, among them Father Jacques Marquette and Louis Jolliet. At the time, American Indians of the Cherokee, Delaware, and Shawnee tribes, among others, lived in Kentucky's forests. The state's name comes from a Cherokee word believed to mean "Meadowland" or "Land of Tomorrow." The state nickname comes from a grass that grows throughout the state. In spring, the grass develops bluish-purple buds that make meadows and lawns look blue.

In 1750, Dr. Thomas Walker, a pioneer scout, entered the Kentucky region through the Cumberland Gap. The Gap is a natural pass through the mountains where Kentucky, Tennessee, and Virginia meet. Walker made the first major exploration of eastern Kentucky. In 1767, Daniel Boone also made an exploration of the area. Two years later, Boone returned and moved into the region. He attempted to bring settlers into the area in 1773, and again in 1775 when they established themselves along the Kentucky River.

Today, Kentucky horse farms around Lexington produce some of the world's finest racehorses. This reputation extends into the state's culture—one of Kentucky's most famous events is the annual Kentucky Derby at Churchill Downs. The natural beauty of Kentucky's outdoor recreational areas, the largest of which is The Land Between the Lakes, attracts many visitors. People looking for automotive history head for the Corvette factory in Bowling Green.

FAMILY FEUD
A stolen pig might not seem like enough to cause two families to feud for several decades—in fact, it was just the first incident in a battle over land and power in the Appalachian Mountains of Kentucky and West Virginia more than a century ago. Today, the Hatfield-McCoy family feud is long over. The two families held a reunion in 1993, and are proud of the marriages and other celebrations they hold together.

DID YOU KNOW?
Kentucky's Mammoth-Flint Ridge caves are the longest cave system in the world. The caves, part of Mammoth Cave National Park, stretch more than 300 miles (483 km).

PIONEER SCOUT DANIEL BOONE
In the mid-1770s, the Transylvania Land Company sent pioneer Daniel Boone to blaze a trail through Kentucky's wilderness. Before then, Boone had visited Kentucky for exploration and hunting, and knew to enter from Virginia through a natural mountain pass called the Cumberland Gap. Boone completed his trail, called Wilderness Road, in 1775. It stretched from the Cumberland Gap to the Kentucky River. After the trail was completed, groups of settlers followed it to settle safely in Kentucky.

THE REAL HORSE COUNTRY

One of the world's most famous racehorses was born in Lexington, Kentucky. Though he only competed for 16 months, Man O' War's record number of wins made him a legend. Many great thoroughbreds are still raised in Kentucky. It's claimed that Kentucky's blue grass gives horses strong, light bones. Thoroughbreds are one of Kentucky's top agricultural products, and can bring the state more than $600 million in revenue each year.

HOME OF THE KENTUCKY DERBY

Louisville's Churchill Downs, with its 1¼-mile (2- km) track is known as the fastest in the world, and is home to the world's best-known horse race. As part of its opening racing program in 1875, it held the first Kentucky Derby. The event is called the "run for the roses" because a blanket of roses—as well as a large cash prize—is presented to the winner. The race is part of the American Triple Crown, which includes Maryland's Preakness Stakes and New York's Belmont Stakes.

OHIO

Ohio River

INDIANA

Ohio

● Louisville

★ FRANKFORT

● Lexington-Fayette

WEST VIRGINIA

KENTUCKY

Mammoth Cave National Park

● Bowling Green

Cumberland Mountains

Cumberland Mountains

APPALACHIAN MOUNTAINS

VIRGINIA

■ *Cumberland Gap*

TENNESSEE

AMERICAN AUTO MAKING

The American Corvette Museum in Bowling Green, Kentucky houses both the first Corvette and the millionth Corvette to roll off the assembly line at the only GM Corvette plant in the world. The plant stands right across the street from the museum.

"THE GREATEST" BOXER

MUHAMMAD ALI

Cassius Marcellus Clay, Jr. was born in Louisville, Kentucky in 1942. At age 18, he won an Olympic gold medal for boxing. Soon after winning the world heavyweight championship in 1964, he joined the Nation of Islam and took the Muslim name of Muhammad Ali. After Ali refused to be drafted into the armed forces in 1967, to fight in the Vietnam War, he was stripped of his title and forced to stop fighting professionally. He began again when a 1971 Supreme Court decision allowed his refusal on religious grounds. He retired in 1981 with a 56-5 record and is the only man ever to win the heavyweight title three times.

Ali said of his fighting style that he "floated like a butterfly and stung like a bee."

THE LAND BETWEEN THE LAKES

Two huge lakes formed by Tennessee Valley Authority-made dams, Kentucky Lake and Lake Barley, have created The Land Between the Lakes. The peninsula between the lakes is one of the country's largest outdoor recreation areas. The area has Kentucky's typical warm summers and cool winters. In January, statewide temperatures average around 36°F (2°C). July temperatures around the state warm up to around 76°F (24°C).

STATE BIRD
Mockingbird

STATE FLOWER
Iris

STATE TREE
Tulip Poplar

CAPITAL
Nashville

POPULATION
5,689,283 (2000)

STATEHOOD
June 1, 1796
Rank: 16th

LARGEST CITIES
Memphis (650,100)
Nashville-Davidson
(569,891)
Knoxville (173,890)

LAND AREA
41,217 sq. mi.
(106,752 sq. km.)

TENNESSEE
the volunteer state

In 1540, Spaniard Hernando de Soto led the first European expedition across the Tennessee River to the Mississippi. No other European explorers entered the area until 1673, when separate visits were made by British and French explorers. At that time, the Cherokee and Chickasaw people, among others, lived in the region. The state's name comes from *Tanasie*, a local Cherokee village.

In 1682, René-Robert Cavelier, Sieur de La Salle, claimed the Mississippi Valley—including present-day Tennessee—for France. The British claimed the land as well, and after the French and Indian War in 1763, the British gained control of the region. New settlers from Virginia and North Carolina came in the late 1700s, but settlement of the area was slow because the Great Smoky Mountains were difficult to cross. After a path was cut through the mountains, white settlement increased rapidly. Thousands of Cherokee, however, were forced off their land to walk the "Trail of Tears" to Oklahoma.

During the War of 1812, Tennessee became known as the Volunteer State because of the number of its men who volunteered and participated in the Battle of New Orleans. Today, Tennessee is home to a variety of wildlife, particularly in Great Smoky Mountain State Park, which has a growing population of red wolves. An equine breed called the Tennessee walking horse has provided the area with financial support, both through breeding in central Tennessee and an annual 11-day celebration of the horses in Shelbyville. The state attracts much of its tourist money and attention as the site of country music's famous Grand Ole Opry and the nation's second most visited home, Elvis Presley's Graceland.

TRAIL OF TEARS
In 1830, President Andrew Jackson signed the Indian Removal Act. The act required the Cherokee to give up their homeland and move west of the Mississippi River. Eight years later, U.S. troops gathered about 14,000 Cherokee men, women, and children from eastern Tennessee, forcing them to walk 1,200 miles (1,931 km) to the plains of Oklahoma along the "Trail of Tears." At least 4,000 Cherokee died on the journey.

TENNESSEE VALLEY AUTHORITY
In 1933, during the Great Depression, President Franklin D. Roosevelt created the Tennessee Valley Authority to produce hydroelectric power from the Tennessee River. This and other public works programs were intended to put people back to work and modernize the region. In Tennessee, a series of dams were built along the river so the water could be used to produce electricity, provide water for nearby crops, and create recreation areas.

KENTUCKY

VIRGINIA

★ NASHVILLE-
DAVIDSON

TENNESSEE

Knoxville

CUMBERLAND MTS

APPALACHIAN MOUNTAINS

Great Smoky
Mountain
State Park

Sweetwater

GREAT SMOKY MTS

• Shelbyville

NORTH CAROLINA

Chattanooga

ALABAMA

GEORGIA

DID YOU KNOW?

Sweetwater, Tennessee's Lost Sea, is the largest underground lake in the U.S. The caverns around the lake were once used by the Cherokee people for meetings.

TENNESSEE WALKING HORSES

Each year in late August, the town of Shelbyville hosts the Tennessee Walking Horse National Celebration. The 11-day event features Tennessee walking horses, renowned for their gentle ride and intelligence.

THE KING OF ROCK AND ROLL'S GRACELAND

Though singer Elvis Presley died in 1977, his fans still flock to his Memphis mansion to tour his home and visit his gravesite. The White House is the only U.S. home to have more visitors. A Trophy Building displays Presley's awards and flashy stage costumes while another building holds his cars, including a pink Cadillac and Harley Davidson golf cart.

MOUNTAIN AND FOREST WILDLIFE

Half of Tennessee is forested and is home to many wild animals, including the red wolf. Because the wolves' numbers had dwindled to almost zero in the wilds of Tennessee and other states, red wolves were reintroduced to Tennessee's Great Smoky Mountain State Park in 1991. The red wolf population now numbers more than 16, and helps control the ecosystem by limiting the number of white-tailed deer.

QUEEN OF SOUL

ARETHA FRANKLIN

Franklin's career has included more than a dozen million-selling singles and 20 Number 1 R&B hits.

Born in Memphis in 1942 to a gospel singer and a reverend, Aretha Franklin and her two sisters sang in the church choir every Sunday while growing up in Detroit, Michigan. At 17, she was encouraged to travel to New York City to record demonstration tapes. Franklin soon had a recording deal with Columbia Records. After six years, 10 albums, and one pop hit, Franklin signed with Atlantic Records. Franklin's powerful singing voice and style enabled her to sell millions of albums with Top 20 hits such as "Chain of Fools" and "Respect." The latter, a call for equal rights for both women and blacks, won her two Grammy awards and a civil rights award from Martin Luther King, Jr.

GREAT SMOKY MOUNTAINS

The Great Smoky Mountains span eastern Tennessee's Blue Ridge region. Their name comes from the mist that is created when the air above the thick, elevated forests mixes with the state's humid climate. Tennessee generally has subtropical weather, although the western half is warmer than the mountain-packed east. Average temperatures range from 71°F (22°C) to 79°F (26°C) in July and between 37°F (3°C) and 40°F (4°C) in January. On average, Tennessee gets 52 inches (132 cm) of precipitation a year, including four to 10 inches (10 to 25 cm) of snow.

STATE BIRD
Cardinal

STATE FLOWER
Dogwood

STATE TREE
Longleaf Pine

CAPITAL
Raleigh

POPULATION
8,049,313 (2000)

STATEHOOD
November 21, 1789
Rank: 12th

LARGEST CITIES
Charlotte (540,828)
Raleigh (276,093)
Greensboro (223,891)

LAND AREA
48,711 sq. mi.
(126,161 sq. km.)

NORTH CAROLINA

the tar heel state

North Carolina and South Carolina were once one large British colony that later split into two states. The colony was called the Province of Carolana, for the Latin name of King Charles I—Carolus.

By the early 1500s, approximately 35,000 American Indians lived in the region. They were members of about 30 tribes, including the Cherokee and the Hatteras. The French and the Spanish both sent expeditions to the region beginning in 1524. In 1584, Sir Walter Raleigh of England tried to establish the area as the first English colony in North America. The colonists settled on Roanoke Island, but returned to England in 1586 after finding life there difficult. The following year, Raleigh sent another group to Roanoke Island under the guidance of English governor John White. Soon after settling, White left the colony to pick up supplies. By the time he returned, almost three years later, the colony was deserted, earning it the nickname "The Lost Colony." In 1650, North Carolina's first permanent settlement of white people was established by colonists from Virginia.

State history is also marked by one of the civil rights movement's defining moments: a 1960 sit-in at a whites-only lunch counter.

Today, the state's popular sites include the furniture manufacturing town of High Point, the mountains and falls of Chimney Rock Park, and the historic towns of Old Salem and Winston-Salem. The Charlotte Speedway's Winston Select all-star car race attracts national attention when it's televised each May.

HISTORIC TOWNS
Tourists are drawn to the twin towns of Winston-Salem for their plantations, which were built on the riches of tobacco and cotton farming. Old Salem is a historic community that has been restored for tourists. Townspeople in period costume guide visitors through more than 100 buildings while a tinsmith, clockmaker, baker, and more demonstrate crafts in the community.

THE LOST COLONY
This 1600s-era map shows the Roanoke Island area. In 1587, Sir Walter Raleigh sent settlers to Roanoke Island, but what happened to them remains a mystery. Among the colonists was governor John White's daughter, Eleanor Dare, who gave birth to a daughter, Virginia. Virginia was the first child to be born to English parents in the American colonies. Soon thereafter, White left for England to pick up necessities. Upon his return in 1590, he was shocked to find the settlement abandoned. To this day, there is no certain information as to what happened to the Roanoke colonists.

VIRGINIA

Eden • • Reidsville
Winston-Salem • • Henderson
• Greensboro
• High Point
Lexington • • Durham
Salisbury •

Roanoke Rapids •
Elizabeth City •
Kill Devil Hills •
Roanoke Island

NORTH CAROLINA

★RALEIGH

• Greenville

Albemarle •
Charlotte •
Monroe •

Goldsboro •
• Kinston
• New Bern

Cape Hatteras National Seashore

Pamlico Sound

Fayetteville •
• Laurinburg
• Lumberton

Havelock •
Jacksonville •

Wilmington •

ATLANTIC OCEAN

FURNITURE CAPITAL OF AMERICA

More than 60 percent of the furniture made in the U.S. is produced in North Carolina. The town of High Point, located near thick oak and pine forests, is nicknamed the Furniture Capital of America. High Point has more than 120 factories that craft tables, chairs, sofas, desks, and more.

DID YOU KNOW?

On December 17, 1903, Wilbur and Orville Wright flew the first successful engine-powered airplane at Kill Devil Hills, near Kitty Hawk, North Carolina.

CIVIL RIGHTS SIT-IN

The Woolworth store in Greensboro, North Carolina became a landmark in the civil rights movement when four black students refused to leave a whites-only lunch counter. On February 1, 1960, the North Carolina A&T State University freshmen—Franklin McCain, David Richmond, Joseph McNeil, and Ezell Blair Jr.—staged a sit-in, refusing to leave even when threatened with arrest. The brave act sparked similar demonstrations by blacks and whites across the then-segregated South. Today Greensboro residents are raising money to turn the store into a museum.

THE BEST IN CAR RACING

Crowds of cheering fans fill the 1.5-mile Lowe's Motor Speedway in Charlotte each May to watch the Winston Select. The NASCAR event is an all-star race open to a special field of only 15 drivers. The Select's winner walks away with a $200,000 prize.

CHARMING FIRST LADY

DOLLEY PAYNE MADISON

Piedmont-born Dolley Payne was a young widow when she met and fell in love with Representative James Madison of Virginia, and they married in 1794. She was the White House hostess for President Thomas Jefferson, a widower, and for her husband, who became president in 1809. In the War of 1812, the British captured Washington and burned the White House. Before the British troops marched in, the First Lady courageously saved a famous painting of George Washington and other treasures.

Madison was said to have greeted friends, her husband's rivals, and heads of state with equal amounts of charm and warmth.

CAPE HATTERAS SEASHORE

Cape Hatteras became the country's first National Seashore in 1953. Located between Nag's Head and Ocracoke Island, the seashore is covered in white sands. Further inland, Cape Hatteras's nature trails provide a hiking path over sand dunes, woodlands, and salt marshes. Temperatures at the cape are warm, but there are also cool ocean breezes. In the southeastern part of the state, July temperatures reach around 80°F (27°C), while January averages 48°F (9°C). The western mountain areas of the state are generally 20°F cooler.

43

SOUTH CAROLINA

the palmetto state

STATE BIRD
Carolina Wren

STATE FLOWER
Yellow Jessamine

STATE TREE
Palmetto

CAPITAL
Columbia

POPULATION
4,012,012 (2000)

STATEHOOD
May 23, 1788
Rank: 8th

LARGEST CITIES
Columbia (116,278)
Charleston (96,650)
North Charleston (79,641)

LAND AREA
30,110 sq. mi.
(77,985 sq. km.)

Taylors • • Greer

Easley • • Greenville

• Anderson

GEORGIA

Greenwood •

More than 30 American Indian cultures, including the Cherokee of the Iroquois family and the Catawaba of the Sioux family, lived in the region before the Spanish, and later the French, tried to colonize the area. In the early 1600s, however, England claimed the South Carolina region, and in 1629, King Charles I granted the lands that now make up North and South Carolina to Sir Robert Heath. The land was named the Province of Carolana in honor of the king. The Latin version of the king's name is Carolus.

OLDEST AFRICAN CRAFT
Sweetgrass baskets are the oldest African-origin craft still made in the Unites States. Sweetgrass is collected along coastal areas and marshlands, and the design of a simple basket can take as much as 12 hours. Sweetgrass has special properties that make the baskets unique; and water will not ruin them.

It wasn't until 1670 that British settlers set up the regions' first permanent settlement at Albemarle Point. In 1710, North and South Carolina were each given their own governor, but the colonies didn't formally separate until 1730.

During the American Revolution, South Carolina was the setting for many major battles. The state was key to the Civil War, having been the first to withdraw from the Union in November, 1860. It was also the site of the war's first attack: On April 12, 1861, Confederate troops fired on Fort Sumter in Charleston Harbor.

Today, South Carolina's economy relies on a variety of industries, including textile manufacturing. The state's natural beauty and cultural events also attract tourists. South Carolina's coastal swamps and estuaries, such as those on Kiawah Island, teem with life—many plant and animal species, such as ancient oaks, sweetgrass, spartina, and salt shrubs; and river otters, loggerhead turtles, and gray foxes, to name just a few.

DID YOU KNOW?

South Carolina has an official state amphibian—the Spotted Salamander, an official state beverage—milk, and an official state dance—the Shag, which originated in Myrtle Beach in the late 1930s.

FIRST CIVIL WAR SITE
On December 20, 1860, South Carolina seceded from the Union. It was the first Southern state to do so. On April 12, 1861, Fort Sumter, a U.S. fort lying at the entrance to Charleston Harbor, was attacked by Confederate forces. For 35 hours, Confederate troops bombarded it with cannon fire. The Union troops surrendered. The attack on Fort Sumter was the first battle of the U.S. Civil War. The granite fort built between 1829 and 1860, became a National Monument in 1948.

BARRIER BEACH

Huntington Beach State Park lies on one of the South Carolina coast's numerous barrier islands. The park is renowned as one of the best birdwatching locales in the United States. Average July temperatures in these areas and in the southern part of the state are around 81°F, while the northwest is a cooler 72°F (27°C). Average January temperatures are a mild 51°F (22°C) in the south and 41°F (5°C) in the northwest.

FROM SWING TO BEBOP

JOHN BIRKS "DIZZY" GILLESPIE

Gillespie taught himself to play trumpet at age 12. By age 23, he was spending his nights jamming with Charlie Parker and Thelonious Monk, among others. Together they developed a fresh, complex style of jazz called bop. After someone fell on his trumpet and bent it in 1953, Gillespie decided he liked the sound the instrument made. From then on, he had all his trumpets manufactured with a 45-degree bend.

Gillespie's nickname was "Dizzy" due to his clownish behavior as a child.

COASTAL SWAMPLANDS

Swamps cover part of the South Carolina coastline and extend inland along rivers. They are home to many unique animals and plants, including cypress trees, which grow out of the swamp floor. One of the state's most famous swamps is the 160-acre (65-hectare) blackwater body at Cypress Gardens, near Charleston.

CLOTHING THE NATION

Textiles, or cloth products, are South Carolina's most important manufactured product. The state now has approximately 500 major mills that develop cotton, silk, wool, polyester, and acrylic. Many of the mills are located in Anderson and Greenwood. Cloth has been big business in South Carolina since the late 1800s when at least 50 textile mills were making cloth. The growth of the industry led to company-owned towns called mill towns. The company owned the mill, the workers' houses, and the grocery store, in addition to supporting the school system.

STATE BIRD
Mockingbird

STATE FLOWER
Apple Blossom

STATE TREE
Pine

CAPITAL
Little Rock

POPULATION
2,673,400 (2000)

STATEHOOD
June 15, 1836
Rank: 25th

LARGEST CITIES
Little Rock (183,133)
Fort Smith (80,268)
North Little Rock (60,433)

LAND AREA
52,068 sq. mi.
(134,856 sq. km.)

ARKANSAS
land of opportunity

Archeological evidence shows that cavedwellers and mound builders, so called because they built enormous ceremonial mounds, were probably the first inhabitants of the area including Arkansas. Hundreds of years later, the first Europeans to enter the area were members of a 1541–42 Spanish expedition by Hernando de Soto. Later, French explorers Father Jacques Marquette and Louis Jolliet sailed down the Mississippi River to the Arkansas River. The Quapaw and Osage were among the American Indian peoples that lived in the area at the time. The state's name is a French translation of a Quapaw term for "land of downstream people."

French lieutenant Henri de Tonti built the first European settlement, Arkansas Post, in 1682. Although René-Robert Cavelier, Sieur de La Salle, had claimed the Mississippi Valley for France, it was put in Spanish hands in 1762 before being ceded to the United States in the Louisiana Purchase of 1803. Arkansas became its own region in 1819, a year after a cotton boom brought in many settlers.

Although the desegregation of white-only schools caused turmoil in the mid-twentieth century, today's forward-thinking Arkansas has retained its distinct culture and crafts, particularly in the Ozark Mountains. Ragtime and blues grew in Arkansas, and events celebrating the roots of those musical styles as well as the area's historic sites attract tourists year-round.

SCHOOL DESEGREGATION
The U.S. Supreme Court ruled that segregation—the separation of blacks and whites in public facilities—was illegal. The first nine black students to enter Little Rock's Central High, in 1957, were met by violent protesters. Under orders by Governor Orval Faubus, Arkansas National Guardsmen turned the Little Rock Nine, as they were called, away from the school. The next day, they returned and were protected by U.S. Army troops, sent by President Eisenhower, as they entered the school.

Fort Smith
National
Historic
Site

HISTORIC GATEWAY
The modern Arkansas-Oklahoma border town of Fort Smith was established as a small fort in late 1817. The fort was nicknamed "Hell on the Border" because it was considered the meeting point of civilization and the untamed West, as neighboring Oklahoma was "Indian Territory." The fort, named for General Thomas Smith, was a gathering place and pass-through point for hunters and trappers during the annual trade rendezvous with American Indians and miners seeking gold in California.

MISSOURI

Jonesboro

ARKANSAS

TENNESSEE

Mississippi River

North Little Rock

★ LITTLE ROCK

Helena

Arkansas River

Mississippi River

MISSISSIPPI

Lake J. Lee

Wilmot

LOUISIANA

WARM, MOIST CLIMATE

Evergreens, such as the lone bald cypress trees at Lake Enterprise near Wilmot and thick forests of Southern pines do well through Arkansas's hot summers and mild winters. July temperatures throughout the state average between 78°F (26°C) and 84°F (29°C), while January temperatures range from 36°F to 46°F (2°C to 8°C). Moisture is generally not a concern, as yearly precipitation averages around 49 inches (124 cm) with 6 inches (15 cm) of snowfall.

CHICKEN AND RICE

One-third of the nation's rice is produced in Arkansas, making it the state's leading crop. The world's largest rice mill is in the town of Jonesboro, and most of the rice processed there comes from the eastern part of the state, where farmers flood their fields to grow rice. Soybeans are the second biggest crop, and Arkansas is the country's fourth largest supplier of cotton. In terms of income, however, broiler chickens are tops.

THE ROOTS OF RAGTIME

SCOTT JOPLIN

Ragtime musician and composer Scott Joplin's work gained its greatest recognition after his death. The Texarkana-raised Joplin, the son of a former slave, was a self-taught pianist who left home in his early teens to work in music. In 1885, the teen settled in St. Louis, Missouri, playing in saloons. Almost a decade later, he began composing ragtime songs. In 1899, he published *Maple Leaf Rag*, an instant hit. In 1976 the Pulitzer Prize Committee awarded Joplin a posthumous prize for his contributions to American music.

Joplin's music grew in popularity when it was featured in the movie The Sting *(1973).*

SINGING THE BLUES

Each year since 1986, the King Biscuit Blues Festival blows into the town of Helena for four days of music and memories. The festival started as a way to honor hometown hero and blues musician Sonny Boy Williamson, who originally performed on a local radio show called the "King Biscuit Hour," sponsored by a flour company of the same name. Today, the festival brings income to the downtown area, which sits in front of a levee holding back the Mississippi River. Crowds of 100,000-plus watch the five stages to hear gospel and blues acts from around the country.

DID YOU KNOW?

The city of Texarkana straddles the Arkansas-Texas border and has separate city governments for each side.

CRYSTAL CLEAR WATERS

Lake Ouachita, surrounded by mountains and nestled in the Ouachita National Forest, is one of the cleanest lakes in the country, according to the Environmental Protection Agency. No homes are allowed in the area, but hikers and campers enjoy its 223-mile (359-km) trail, 1,000 miles (1,609 km) of shoreline, and more than 200 islands. One part of the artificially created lake is so clean that it is home to rare non-stinging jellyfish and sponges as well as more common striped bass and catfish. Elsewhere, the state's landscape is filled with mountains, rolling valleys, mineral springs, and fertile plains.

MISSISSIPPI

the magnolia state

The American Indians who once lived in Mississippi included the Chickasaw in the north, the Choctaw in the south–central region, and the Natchez in the southwest. Many were struck down in large numbers by diseases carried by members of Spanish explorer Hernando de Soto's expedition into the area in about 1540. France claimed the region in 1682, but the French, British, Spanish, and American Indians continued to fight for control until 1812, when the U.S. took possession of the region. The state's name is borrowed from the mighty river that bounds the state on the west.

Cotton was king in Mississippi in the nineteenth century, and slave labor was used to provide huge profits to plantation owners. This slave-based economy led Mississippians to join the South's efforts to secede from the Union, leading to the Civil War.

Mississippi's economy slowly recovered from the devastation of the war, in part by developing its industrial sector and diversifying its agricultural output to include soybeans, rice, and corn. Mississippi farmers enjoy a long growing season with bountiful rainfall and mild winters with very little snow. Hurricanes are a danger, especially on the Gulf Coast, where crops are cultivated year-round. Mississippi is a largely rural state with a distinctive regional culture that has produced nationally known writers and musicians.

DID YOU KNOW?

The story goes that President Theodore Roosevelt went hunting in Mississippi in 1902, and refused to shoot a captured bear cub. From this tale came the teddy bear.

VICKSBURG BATTLEFIELD

Civil War memorials, including the Union cemetery at Vicksburg, abound in Mississippi. During the Civil War, Union forces tried to capture this Confederate-controlled port city several times before Union General Ulysses S. Grant finally succeeded. Grant's forces laid siege to Vicksburg for more than six weeks before Confederate General John C. Pemberton surrendered on July 4, 1863. Grant's victory at Vicksburg marked a key turning point in the war, but came at a terrible cost, with more than 20,000 men killed or wounded.

THE MIGHTY MISSISSIPPI

The Mississippi River serves as the state's western boundary, and the fertile lowlands adjacent to the river, or floodplains, are known as the Delta. Central Mississippi boasts rolling prairies with soil so rich and black it has come to be known as the "Black Belt." The fabled cotton plantations of the pre-Civil War South flourished here.

WILLIAM FAULKNER

Novelist, short-story writer, and screenwriter William Faulkner chronicled everyday life in Mississippi and explored the legacy of slavery and poverty in the Deep South. Faulkner's work was critically acclaimed and earned him a Nobel Prize in 1949. The award brought him a wide readership and a role as an international speaker and activist. His work is regarded as among America's best literature.

Most of Faulkner's novels are set in the imaginary county of Yoknapatawpha, Mississippi.

MUDDY WATERS

Muddy Waters, the legendary blues musician, is one of the many artists whose life and works are chronicled at the Delta Blues Museum in Clarksdale, Mississippi. The Mississippi Delta is considered a birthplace of the blues, African-American folk music that originated in the early 1900s. Blues, which were inspired in part by the pain and suffering endured by enslaved African-Americans, later influenced the development of popular music—including rock-and-roll.

A RURAL POPULATION

Mississippi has one of the largest rural populations in the U.S.—about half its people live in the countryside and small towns. The rhythms of small-town life predominate and make Mississippi a popular tourist destination for those seeking a respite from urban crowding. The state also has the nation's highest proportion of African-Americans in its population—nearly 37 percent.

CATFISH FARM

Workers repair nets at a catfish farm in Mississippi. The state is the national leader in farm-raised catfish. Shrimp and oyster fishing off Mississippi's coast on the Gulf of Mexico also generates high income for the state. And with more than 40,000 farms operating in the state, agriculture also remains important to the state's economy, with livestock, cotton, and soybeans the chief products. Industry in Mississippi is highly diversified and includes food processing, shipbuilding, and timber and wood processing.

OLD SOUTH MEETS NEW

Large cotton plantations based on slave labor supported a wealthy few whose legendary society was largely destroyed by the Civil War. Today this chapter in Mississippi's history is commemorated with restored plantations, festivals, and events such as the Natchez Ball that re-create life in the "Old South."

ALABAMA

GULF OF MEXICO

● Biloxi

fport

STATE FACTS

STATE BIRD
Yellowhammer

STATE FLOWER
Camellia

STATE TREE
Southern Pine

CAPITAL
Montgomery

POPULATION
4,447,100 (2000)

STATEHOOD
December 14, 1819
Rank: 22nd

LARGEST CITIES
Birmingham (242,820)
Montgomery (201,568)
Mobile (198,915)

LAND AREA
50,744 sq. mi.
(131,427 sq. km.)

ALABAMA
the cotton state

The Choctaw, who lived in present-day southwestern Alabama, were also the source of the state's name, which means "thicket clearers." The Chickasaw, Cherokee, and Creek also lived in the region when Spanish explorers came in search of gold in the early 1500s. The French established the region's first permanent settlements in the early 1700s and claimed the region, despite competing claims by the Spanish and English.

In 1803, the U.S. gained control of the area with the Louisiana Purchase. Disputes with the Spanish and with American Indians were not resolved until 1814, however. Meanwhile, settlers from the U.S. flocked to the region to farm cotton.

Though most Alabama cotton farmers did not own slaves, they believed in that right and felt their way of life was threatened by Northern abolitionists, who wanted to end slavery. Alabama seceded from the Union in January 1861, and Montgomery served as the Confederacy's first capital. After the war, Alabamans struggled to diversify their economy, and Birmingham emerged as a center of the iron and steel industry.

Today, Alabama's diversified agricultural sector is balanced by a strong industrial base, which includes the manufacture of paper products and textiles. Alabama's agricultural and tourist industries benefit from the region's subtropical climate; its long, warm summers and short, mild winters offer a lengthy growing season and mild weather.

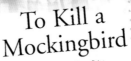

To Kill a Mockingbird
Winner of the Pulitzer Prize

TO KILL A MOCKINGBIRD
The Pulitzer-Prize-winning and nationally beloved novel *To Kill a Mockingbird* (1960) tells the tragic story of a black man falsely accused of assaulting a white woman. Alabama native and author Harper Lee loosely based the novel on her memories of the 1931 Alabama case of the "Scottsboro Nine."

TUSKEGEE UNIVERSITY
Tuskegee University is a historically black college founded by educator Booker T. Washington. For its first four decades, it provided African-Americans with occupational training, which was available to them at few other places. The school then became an accredited college and still later a university. Many notable African-American scholars and leaders have been educated at or employed by Tuskegee, including scientist George Washington Carver. Today, this university is home to more than 3,000 students and is also a national historic site.

MOBILE MOBILITY

Located at the mouth of the Mobile River on Mobile Bay, the city of Mobile is Alabama's only major seaport and has played a central role in the state's industrial and commercial life. The Alabama State Docks in Mobile are the nation's second largest exporter of coal and other goods that include oil, iron, and chemicals. The importance of waterways to Mobile's history and development can also be seen in the thriving shipbuilding and repair trade.

SPACE CAMP

Huntsville is home to the U. S. Space & Rocket Center, which uses its impressive collection of high-tech weaponry, rockets, and other spacecraft to provide an interactive history of the U.S. space program. The center offers "Space Camp" for visitors of all ages, who spend several days undergoing astronaut training much like that of actual astronauts.

DID YOU KNOW?

The first Mardi Gras celebration held in the United States took place in Mobile, Alabama, in 1704. It is still celebrated there today.

PLENTIFUL PEANUTS

Cotton was king in Alabama until 1915, when an infestation of boll weevils decimated the crop and forced farmers to diversify and adopt new farming techniques to protect the soil and their crops. Today, peanuts, corn, and soybeans are grown in fields once devoted entirely to cotton, and much cropland was turned into pastureland for beef and dairy cattle. Chicken, beef cattle, and other livestock make up the leading source of Alabama's farm income.

GO FOR THE GULF COAST

Northern Alabama is mountainous terrain, marked with ridges, plateaus, and many river valleys. Traveling southward, the elevation drops and gives way to the rolling grasslands of the Black Belt and then swampy lowlands on the Gulf Coast. Today, Alabama's Gulf Coast is a popular vacation spot with its sandy beaches, rich recreational fishing areas, and many historic sites to satisfy the needs of all its visitors.

COURAGEOUS ADVOCATE

HELEN KELLER

Educator, author, and activist Helen Keller was born on June 27, 1880 in Tuscumbia, Alabama. At the age of 19 months, she became deaf, blind, and mute due to an illness. Her disabilities made education a major challenge, and in 1887 she began working with Anne Sullivan, a teacher for the blind. Keller learned sign language, to read Braille, write, and also speak. She went on to graduate with honors from Radcliffe College in 1904.

Keller spent her life working to provide adequate and innovative education and equal treatment for disabled people around the world.

STATE FACTS

STATE BIRD
Brown Thrasher

STATE FLOWER
Cherokee Rose

STATE TREE
Live Oak

CAPITAL
Atlanta

POPULATION
8,186,453 (2000)

STATEHOOD
January 2, 1788
Rank: 4th

LARGEST CITIES
Atlanta (416,474)
Augusta-Richmond
(199,775)
Columbus (186,291)

LAND AREA
57,906 sq. mi.
(149,977 sq. km.)

GEORGIA
the peach state

Europeans first saw the coast of Georgia during Spanish explorer Hernando de Soto's 1539 voyage. By that time, the Creek and Cherokee had been cultivating corn, beans, and tobacco in the region for hundreds of years. The land, which would be named for the English king George II, eventually fell to British rule, and was one of the original 13 colonies.

Georgia's varied landscape and warm, humid weather was ideal for raising both rice and cotton. The agrarian economy that developed was based on slave labor. Between the American Revolution and the Civil War, Georgia's population and economy boomed when cotton became a profitable cash crop. The hunger for more farmland led to the forced removal of Georgia's native population on a march known as the "Trail of Tears," which led to the deaths of nearly 4,000 Cherokee and Creek.

During the Civil War, the Union's attempt to ruin Georgia's economy led to the destruction of its transportation network. With the Union victory, Georgia and the rest of the South faced the awesome task of rebuilding.

Today, manufacturing, service industries, and retail trade provide livelihoods for most Georgians, although farming is still important to the economy.

TENNESSEE

BLUE RIDGE MOUNTAINS

ATLANTA ★

ALABAMA

● Columbus

PICK A PEACH
Georgia is known as the peach state, and produces more than $27 million worth of peaches each year. Cotton, however, is still among the state's most important crops. Georgia's wide-ranging topography and climate means the state's growers can offer up an assortment of fruit, including watermelon, peaches, and tomatoes.

ANDERSONVILLE
The use of slave labor on farms and plantations throughout the South led to political and social conflict with Northern states, and, eventually, the Civil War. In February 1864, a prison camp for Union soldiers opened near the village of Andersonville, Georgia. Lacking adequate food, shelter, or medical care, nearly 13,000 soldiers died at the camp in little more than a year. Today, the Georgia Monument in Andersonville honors all U.S. prisoners of war.

BURIAL FIGURINES
American Indians settled in Georgia as early as 1,200 years ago and built their settlements around large ceremonial mounds that were used for worship, rituals, and burials. The immense structures were often filled with artwork, pottery, and figurines, such as these, which were found at the Etowah Indian Mounds Historic Site.

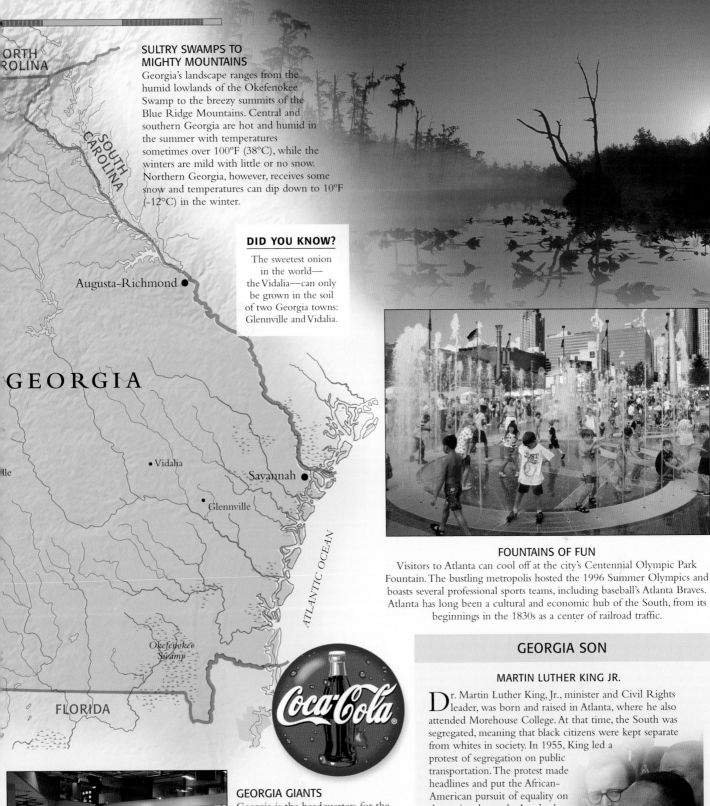

SULTRY SWAMPS TO MIGHTY MOUNTAINS

Georgia's landscape ranges from the humid lowlands of the Okefenokee Swamp to the breezy summits of the Blue Ridge Mountains. Central and southern Georgia are hot and humid in the summer with temperatures sometimes over 100°F (38°C), while the winters are mild with little or no snow. Northern Georgia, however, receives some snow and temperatures can dip down to 10°F (-12°C) in the winter.

DID YOU KNOW?

The sweetest onion in the world— the Vidalia—can only be grown in the soil of two Georgia towns: Glennville and Vidalia.

NORTH CAROLINA

SOUTH CAROLINA

Augusta-Richmond ●

GEORGIA

● Vidalia

Savannah ●

● Glennville

ATLANTIC OCEAN

Okefenokee Swamp

FLORIDA

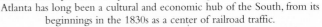

FOUNTAINS OF FUN

Visitors to Atlanta can cool off at the city's Centennial Olympic Park Fountain. The bustling metropolis hosted the 1996 Summer Olympics and boasts several professional sports teams, including baseball's Atlanta Braves. Atlanta has long been a cultural and economic hub of the South, from its beginnings in the 1830s as a center of railroad traffic.

GEORGIA SON

MARTIN LUTHER KING JR.

Dr. Martin Luther King, Jr., minister and Civil Rights leader, was born and raised in Atlanta, where he also attended Morehouse College. At that time, the South was segregated, meaning that black citizens were kept separate from whites in society. In 1955, King led a protest of segregation on public transportation. The protest made headlines and put the African-American pursuit of equality on the national agenda. As a leader of the Civil Rights movement, King led voter-registration campaigns throughout the South as well as the 1963 march on Washington where he delivered his "I Have a Dream" speech.

Martin Luther King at the Civil Rights March on Washington in August of 1963.

GEORGIA GIANTS

Georgia is the headquarters for the Cable News Network (CNN), a major news outlet, as well as for many industries, including lumber, banking, and insurance. One famous Georgia product dates back to 1886, when an Atlanta pharmacist began selling a cure for many common illnesses— Coca Cola. Established in 1892, the Coca Cola Company, one of the nation's soft-drink giants, remains headquartered in Atlanta. Today, its products are known and sold throughout the world.

STATE FACTS

STATE BIRD
Brown Pelican

STATE FLOWER
Magnolia

STATE TREE
Bald Cypress

CAPITAL
Baton Rouge

POPULATION
4,468,976 (2000)

STATEHOOD
April 30, 1812
Rank: 18th

LARGEST CITIES
New Orleans (484,674)
Baton Rouge (227,818)
Shreveport (200,145)

LAND AREA
43,562 sq. mi.
(112,826 sq. km.)

LOUISIANA
the pelican state

With an abundance of natural resources and a desirable geographical location at the site where the mighty Mississippi River empties into the Gulf of Mexico, Louisiana was a hotly contested territory. Many American Indian groups lived in the region, including the Choctaw along the Mississippi and the Chitimacha in the southern coastal region. The French and Spanish vied for control of the region in the 1700s, and these settlers established the distinctive Creole and Cajun cultures, which continue to flourish in the region to this day. French explorers named the region for King Louis XIV.

By 1810, the U.S. government had gained control of all of present-day Louisiana, which became a state in 1812. The state's subtropical climate—brief, mild winters with little snow or ice and long, hot, humid summers—as well as its rich soil, have made it a center for the cultivation of cotton, sugarcane, and rice. The fertile land drew many settlers, particularly from other parts of the South.

The sugar and cotton plantations in Louisiana depended upon slave labor, and the state seceded from the Union and joined the Confederacy on the eve of the Civil War. In the twentieth century, the extraction of oil and natural gas helped to diversify the state's economy. Today the mining, farming, fishing, lumber, and tourism industries all contribute to the state's economy, which is anchored by the port city of New Orleans and its considerable manufacturing, educational, and cultural resources.

Shreveport

Driskill Mountain

TEXAS

LOU

THE CAPTURE OF NEW ORLEANS

Shortly after Louisiana became a state on April 30, 1812, the United States and Great Britain went to war. In the fall of 1814, British troops prepared for a naval invasion of New Orleans in an effort to gain control of the Mississippi River, which served as an important trade and supply route. The U.S., led by General Andrew Jackson, defeated the British. Neither side realized that the war had ended several weeks previously—the news had not yet reached New Orleans.

MARDI GRAS

New Orleans's Mardi Gras is famous throughout the world. People from all faiths and walks of life join in the celebration, participating in parades, masked balls, and folk dances. Mardi Gras, which means "Fat Tuesday," is the day before Ash Wednesday in the Christian Easter season.

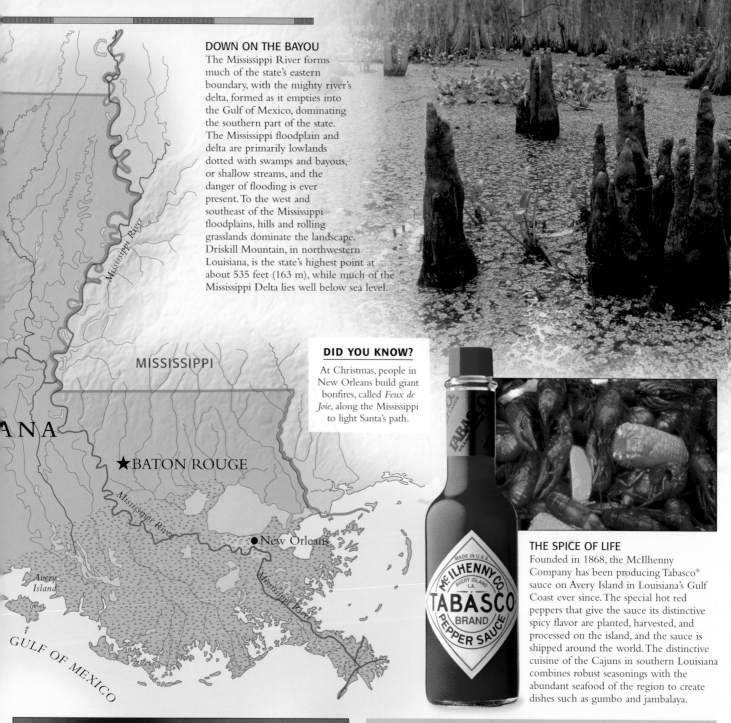

DOWN ON THE BAYOU

The Mississippi River forms much of the state's eastern boundary, with the mighty river's delta, formed as it empties into the Gulf of Mexico, dominating the southern part of the state. The Mississippi floodplain and delta are primarily lowlands dotted with swamps and bayous, or shallow streams, and the danger of flooding is ever present. To the west and southeast of the Mississippi floodplains, hills and rolling grasslands dominate the landscape. Driskill Mountain, in northwestern Louisiana, is the state's highest point at about 535 feet (163 m), while much of the Mississippi Delta lies well below sea level.

DID YOU KNOW?

At Christmas, people in New Orleans build giant bonfires, called *Feux de Joie*, along the Mississippi to light Santa's path.

MISSISSIPPI

★BATON ROUGE

Mississippi River

●New Orleans

Avery Island

Mississippi River

GULF OF MEXICO

THE SPICE OF LIFE

Founded in 1868, the McIlhenny Company has been producing Tabasco® sauce on Avery Island in Louisiana's Gulf Coast ever since. The special hot red peppers that give the sauce its distinctive spicy flavor are planted, harvested, and processed on the island, and the sauce is shipped around the world. The distinctive cuisine of the Cajuns in southern Louisiana combines robust seasonings with the abundant seafood of the region to create dishes such as gumbo and jambalaya.

SWEET ABUNDANCE

When sugarcane is ready to be harvested, the farmer sets fire to the field. This process destroys the plant's leaves, leaving the cane, with its thick shell, intact. The state's climate provides optimal growing conditions for this crop, making Louisiana a national leader in its production. Louisiana's farmers also cultivate cotton, rice, and soybeans.

LOUISIANA SON

LOUIS ARMSTRONG

Louis Armstrong first learned his craft on the streets and in the clubs of his hometown, New Orleans. He became a major innovator in the jazz world and, in the 1930s, helped shape the emerging musical style called swing. Armstrong drew upon a wide variety of American music—from blues to popular standards—to develop his art form. He also broke through many racial barriers in the entertainment world, performing on the radio, in films, on television, and in live performances at a time when few blacks were given such opportunities.

Armstrong was called "Satchmo" because of his childhood nickname, "Satchel Mouth."

STATE FACTS

STATE BIRD
Mockingbird

STATE FLOWER
Orange Blossom

STATE TREE
Palmetto Palm

CAPITAL
Tallahassee

POPULATION
15,982,378 (2000)

STATEHOOD
March 3, 1845
Rank: 27th

LARGEST CITIES
Jacksonville (735,617)
Miami (362,470)
Tampa (303,447)

LAND AREA
53,927 sq. mi.
(139,671 sq. km.)

FLORIDA
the sunshine state

The first European sighting of the long, low-lying peninsula of Florida came six years after Christopher Columbus's first voyage to the Americas. In 1498, John and Sebastian Cabot spotted Cape Florida on Key Biscayne in what is now Miami. At the time the land had an estimated 100,000 inhabitants, including the Timucua and the Apalachee peoples. In 1513, Juan Ponce de Leon sailed to the region during Spain's spring holiday, *Pascua Florida*, the Feast of the Flowers. He came ashore and named the land La Florida in honor of the holiday.

More Spaniards settled in St. Augustine in 1565. These settlers and visiting British explorers clashed with American Indians throughout the 1500s and 1600s. By the 1700s, many remaining tribes joined the Seminole, who had recently migrated from Georgia. The Seminole were later pushed out of central Florida by the U.S. Army. Florida was an attractive piece of land because of its strategic location, and also for its warm, wet climate and rich soil.

Today, Florida's climate attracts many older citizens and tourists, who enjoy its beaches, amusement parks, historical sites, and lush landscape, which also provides a home for unique animal species such as the flamingo. High-tech companies, as well as the National Aeronautics and Space Administration (NASA), have flocked to the state to take advantage of its skilled work force and temperate weather.

DID YOU KNOW?
The sports drink Gatorade was developed at the University of Florida and is named for the football team.

SETTLING ST. AUGUSTINE
King Phillip II of Spain asked Pedro Menendez de Aviles to be Florida's governor in 1565. Menendez and his soldiers arrived in Florida on August 28, 1565, the Feast Day of St. Augustine. Days later, they took over the Timucuan Indian village of Seloy and renamed it St. Augustine. It was the first permanent European settlement in what would become the U.S.

HEMINGWAY'S HOUSE
Nobel Prize-winning author Ernest Hemingway lived at his Key West home from 1900 to his death in 1961 and wrote his novel *For Whom the Bell Tolls* there. In the 1930s, the house gained attention as the site of the small island's first swimming pool. The house has new occupants now—at least 60 cats. Hemingway was given a six-toed cat by a friend, and many of the cats that live on the grounds today are that cat's offspring. Every year a litter or two of kittens are born, ensuring that Hemingway's cats remain permanent residents.

AMPLE ANIMALS
Florida's sunny setting is often symbolized by the flamingo, but today this colorful shrimp-eating bird is only common in zoos and parks. Approximately 150 species of reptiles and amphibians, such as American crocodiles and alligators, green sea turtles, and eastern coral snakes, also live in Florida. Ninety species of mammals, including Florida panthers, black bears, manatees, and bottle-nosed dolphins, also coexist. Add to this hundreds of bird and fish species, most of which feed in the rich wetlands. In the last few decades, as land in northern and central Florida has been developed, many species of wildlife have moved south toward the Gulf Coast.

GEORGIA

★ TALLAHASSEE

Jacksonville

St. Augustine

Gulf of Mexico

ATLANTIC OCEAN

Daytona
Beach

Orlando

FLORIDA

Walt
Disney
World

Kennedy
Space
Center

Tampa

Saint Petersburg

*Lake
Okeechobee*

Fort
Lauderdale

Miami

The Everglades

Florida Keys

Key West

HIS PEOPLE'S LEADER

OSCEOLA

Osceola was born a Creek Indian and a native of Alabama, but he later became a leader of the Seminole people who took refuge in Florida. As increasing white settlement pushed native people farther south and west, the Seminole had been forced from their ancestral lands in Georgia. Osceola led his people in the Second Seminole War (1835–1842), but died as a captive of the U.S. army on January 30, 1838.

An artist who painted Osceola's portrait called him "a most extraordinary man…a cunning and restless spirit."

YEAR-ROUND TOURISM

Tourism is the state's largest income-producer, and with attractions like Walt Disney World, it's no wonder. In 1999, more than 58.9 million visitors came to Florida for business and pleasure, which brought in $46.7 billion.

SWEET CITRUS

Agriculture is the state's second biggest industry after tourism, and citrus fruit is key. Oranges, grapefruit, tangerines, and about 1.5 billion gallons of their juices bring in about $8 billion each year. The state's 70 million citrus trees produce much of the world's citrus fruit.

KLINK CITRUS
IVANHOE
COR 49603 CLIN

KLINK CITRUS
IVANHOE
COR 49603 CLIN

HIGH FLYING HIGH-TECH

Thousands of spectators gather at Cape Canaveral in the early dawn before every shuttle launch. Passes to view the launch in person are difficult to come by, so many more watch the missions rocket into the stratosphere from boats and cars. Since 1958, NASA's space center has been the launch site for many important missions, including the July 16, 1969, Moon landing. Many defense and research companies are located on or near Cape Canaveral, taking advantage of the area's high-tech manufacturing facilities. Tampa and Pensacola are among the cities that have major air and naval facilities.

EVERGREEN EVERGLADES

Once a free-flowing river with Lake Okeechobee as its source, a dam now holds much of the Everglades's waters back. The swampland is shallow and covered in some parts by tall sawgrass, limestone rock, and tree islands known as hammocks. Its wetlands provide food and shelter for many wild animals, some of which are unique to the area.

THE MIDWEST STATES

Five of the eight Midwest states—Ohio, Indiana, Illinois, Michigan, and Wisconsin—were carved out of the Northwest Territory, which was formed in 1787 from land ceded by the British to the newly formed U.S. at the end of the American Revolution. Minnesota, Iowa, and Missouri were acquired from France in the 1803 Louisiana Purchase. Canals built in the 1820s and 1830s allowed white settlers to reach North America's interior more easily. Their arrival, however, meant battle, defeat, and resettlement for American Indians.

Much of the Midwest's considerable harvest of corn, wheat, and other grains is processed in the region and then shipped all over the nation and the world.

The region served as a gateway to the West as well as becoming home to farmers, merchants, and others. By the late 1800s, railroads built across America made Chicago the industrial and commercial center of the Midwest; other cities also grew quickly. Today, the region is a leading producer of corn, wheat, grain, soybeans, and many other products that feed the world. Automobiles and electronics are important products of this area, too.

CLIMATE

The Midwest enjoys four distinct seasons with cold, snowy winters and humid summers. Abrupt weather changes, however, can be caused by the collision of warm, moist air from the Gulf of Mexico with the jet stream—dry, cold air from Canada. In the winter, this can cause blizzards, while in spring it can cause severe thunderstorms and tornadoes. The region's growing season lasts from April through October.

The jet stream causes weather patterns to change quickly throughout the Midwest.

KEY DATES

1784–7 The Northwest Territory is organized and opened for settlement by the U.S. Ohio, Indiana, Illinois, Michigan, and Wisconsin are later carved out of this territory.

1825 New York's Erie Canal opens. This transportation network allows goods and people to flow from the crowded Northeast to the sparsely inhabited Midwest.

1860 Abraham Lincoln, a senator from Illinois, is elected president. The Southern states begin to secede from the Union, sparking the Civil War.

LANDSCAPE

The Midwest is noted for its flat and gently rolling plains, which include the grass-covered prairies of north-central Iowa, Illinois, and western Indiana. Glaciers covered much of the region during the last Ice Age, which ended about 10,000 years ago. Erosion caused by the glacier's retreat helped create the landscape, as well as giving the area with rich soil excellent for farming. Iowa and Missouri are the only landlocked states in the region; the rest have shoreline on four of the five Great Lakes, which offer ports, considerable scenic beauty, and an abundance of wildlife and vegetation. The Mississippi and Missouri Rivers are also important travel and trade routes and are just two of the many rivers that traverse the region. Minnesota, the "Land of 10,000 Lakes," actually boasts more than 15,000, which provide ample opportunity for outdoor recreation of all kinds.

Skiers cross the finish line in Wisconsin's cross-country ski marathon, the American Birkebeiner. Devotees of winter recreational sports can find much to do in America's Midwest.

LIFESTYLE

The American Birkebeiner, North America's largest cross-country skiing marathon, is run every year from Hayward to Cable, Wisconsin. This celebration of the region's Scandinavian heritage also typifies the rich cultural and recreational offerings of the Midwest. St. Louis's historic St. Charles district provides a glimpse of rough-and-tumble settler life in the early 1800s. The Lincoln Heritage Trail, which passes through Indiana and Illinois, is a 2,200-mile (3,540-km) tour of sites important to the life of President Abraham Lincoln. The Trail follows the travels of Lincoln's frontier family, finally ending at his Springfield, Illinois, home. Minnesota's Mall of America is the nation's largest retail and entertainment center. Meanwhile, the Indianapolis Motor Speedway is one of the world's premier auto racing sites. Truly there is something for everyone in America's heartland.

ECONOMY

The Midwest is a region known for its highly diversified economy, with high levels of industrial and agricultural production. Major commercial, industrial, and cultural urban centers like Chicago and Minneapolis–St. Paul and rich farmlands, including the plains of southern Wisconsin and the prairies of Iowa, have made the Midwest an agricultural storehouse as well as an industrial powerhouse. Automobile manufacturing is important throughout the region, with Detroit serving as the nation's capital in this industry. The Midwest is not only a center for the production of transportation equipment; these states also serve as a transportation link for the nation, with numerous ports on the Great Lakes and the mighty Mississippi and miles of railroad tracks and interstate highways. Indiana's state motto, "The Crossroads of America," is a good description of the entire region.

Chicago is the nation's third-largest city, with a population of almost three million. As the birthplace of the skyscraper, the city boasts an impressive skyline and many architectural treasures.

1899 Michigan's first car factory is established in Lansing by Ransom E. Olds. Other automakers follow, including Ford and General Motors.

1911 The first Indianapolis 500 takes place on Memorial Day. The winner takes nearly seven hours to finish the race.

1973 Chicago's Sears Tower is completed, making it the tallest building in the world. Today, this Illinois building remains the tallest building in the U.S.

1992 The Mall of America opens in Bloomington, Minnesota. It is the largest retail and entertainment center in the U.S.

STATE FACTS

STATE BIRD
Common Loon

STATE FLOWER
Pink and White
Lady's Slipper

STATE TREE
Red (Norway) Pine

CAPITAL
St. Paul

POPULATION
4,919,479 (2000)

STATEHOOD
May 11, 1858
Rank: 32nd

LARGEST CITIES
Minneapolis (382,618)
St. Paul (287,151)
Duluth (86,918)

LAND AREA
79,610 sq. mi.
(206,190 sq. km.)

MINNESOTA
land of 10,000 lakes

The word *Minnesota* comes from the Dakota term meaning "cloudy or sky-tinted water"—an appropriate name since the state has more than 15,000 lakes. The Dakota, or Sioux, were descendants of the Mississippian mound-building culture that thrived from about 800 B.C. to A.D. 1300. In the 1600s, the Ojibwa moved into the northern and eastern woodlands of Minnesota from Ohio and points farther east.

Minnesota has two distinctive landscapes: the vast woodlands of its north and east give way to rolling grasslands known as prairies. The state weather ranges widely from north to south, with average summer temperatures of 60°F and 74°F (16°C and 23°C) respectively. The state's long, cold winters are snowy, too—30 inches (76 cm) of snow fall per year in the west and 70 inches (178 cm) in the northeast. American Indians, fur traders, and soldiers constituted most of the territory's population until the 1850s, when the U.S. took over native lands. At that time, settlers seeking fertile farmland arrived from the eastern U.S., Scandinavia, and Germany.

After entering the Union in 1858, Minnesota's economy was driven by farming, logging, and mining. Today food production and processing, dairy farming, manufacturing of industrial and electronic equipment, publishing, and tourism contribute greatly to the state's economy.

CRY WOLF
The gray wolf became an endangered species in 1974. Today, Minnesota's gray wolf population is thriving thanks to intensive state conservation efforts and the creation of many wildlife refuges.

THE MIGHTY MISSISSIPPI BEGINS
Lake Itasca in central Minnesota is the source of the Mississippi River, one of the most important commercial waterways in the world. The Mississippi's headwaters meander through central and southern Minnesota, and the navigable head of the river, where boats can travel, is at St. Paul. In prehistoric Minnesota, glaciers scoured the land, forming prairies in the western half of the state. They also helped create the numerous lakes that give the state its nickname—the Land of 10,000 Lakes.

DAKOTA UPRISING
As the fur trade and timber industries grew, white settlement in the 1800s remained slow until land treaties were negotiated with the Dakota and Ojibwa. Tensions led to bloodshed when the treaties' terms were not honored by whites. In 1862 Dakota forces, led by Chief Little Crow, attacked the settlers (pictured above). U.S. military forces then drove most of the Dakota westward.

CANADA

NORTH DAKOTA

SOUTH DAKOTA

Red River of the North

Upper Red

Lower Red L

M I N

Itasca State Park

Lake Itasca

Minnesota River

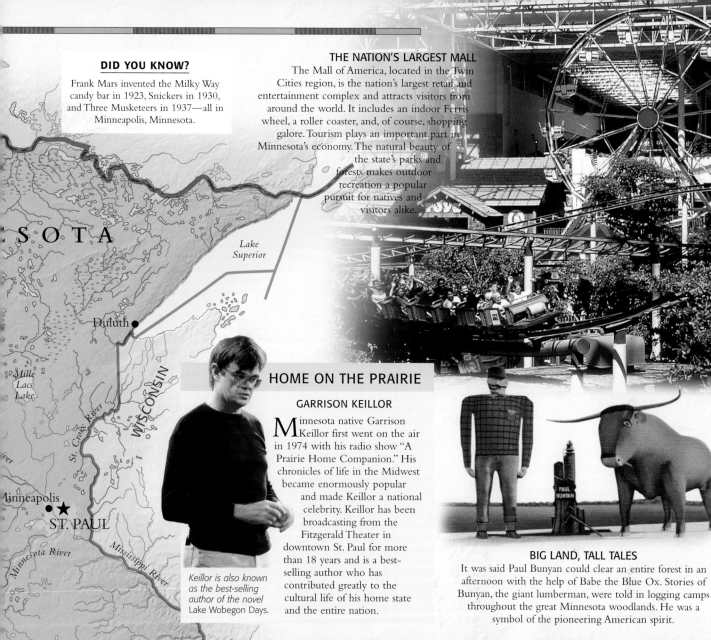

DID YOU KNOW?

Frank Mars invented the Milky Way candy bar in 1923, Snickers in 1930, and Three Musketeers in 1937—all in Minneapolis, Minnesota.

THE NATION'S LARGEST MALL

The Mall of America, located in the Twin Cities region, is the nation's largest retail and entertainment complex and attracts visitors from around the world. It includes an indoor Ferris wheel, a roller coaster, and, of course, shopping galore. Tourism plays an important part in Minnesota's economy. The natural beauty of the state's parks and forests makes outdoor recreation a popular pursuit for natives and visitors alike.

HOME ON THE PRAIRIE

GARRISON KEILLOR

Minnesota native Garrison Keillor first went on the air in 1974 with his radio show "A Prairie Home Companion." His chronicles of life in the Midwest became enormously popular and made Keillor a national celebrity. Keillor has been broadcasting from the Fitzgerald Theater in downtown St. Paul for more than 18 years and is a best-selling author who has contributed greatly to the cultural life of his home state and the entire nation.

Keillor is also known as the best-selling author of the novel Lake Wobegon Days.

BIG LAND, TALL TALES

It was said Paul Bunyan could clear an entire forest in an afternoon with the help of Babe the Blue Ox. Stories of Bunyan, the giant lumberman, were told in logging camps throughout the great Minnesota woodlands. He was a symbol of the pioneering American spirit.

SHIP CENTRAL

Duluth, located on the shores of Lake Superior, has existed as a shipping center since the late 1600s, during the early days of the fur trade. Today, grains produced in northwestern Minnesota and points farther west, as well as iron ore mined in the northeastern part of the state, pass through this bustling port.

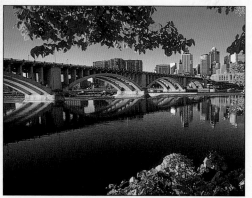

THE TWIN CITIES

St. Paul—the state capital—and Minneapolis are known as the Twin Cities. They lie across the Mississippi River from each other and form the first major port on the mighty river. This metropolitan region is the state's center for trade, transportation, industry, and commerce. Private and public colleges and universities abound, including the main campus of the state-run University of Minnesota system, contributing to the rich cultural life of the region.

WHOLE LOT OF HOTDOG

Established in 1891, Hormel Foods Corporation is still headquartered in Austin, Minnesota, and continues to produce a wide range of foods, including Spam,® for markets around the world. Here, workers create the world's longest hot dog.

STATE FACTS

STATE BIRD
Robin

STATE FLOWER
Wood Violet

STATE TREE
Sugar Maple

CAPITAL
Madison

POPULATION
5,363,675 (2000)

STATEHOOD
May 29, 1848
Rank: 30th

LARGEST CITIES
Milwaukee (596,974)
Madison (208,054)
Green Bay (102,313)
Kenosha (90,352)

LAND AREA
54,310 sq. mi.
(140,663 sq. km.)

WISCONSIN

1848

WISCONSIN
the badger state

The word *Wisconsin* is derived from the French translation of an Ojibwa word meaning "the place where we live" or "gathering of the waters," and became the name of a river and then the state. Wisconsin's first settlers were Paleo-Indians who entered the region 12,000 years ago. By the late 1600s, when French fur traders and missionaries began establishing forts and trading posts, the Ojibwa, Dakota (Sioux), and Potawatomi were among the many American Indians inhabiting what would become Wisconsin.

Once the U.S. established complete control of the region in the 1810s, the discovery of rich mineral deposits sparked massive white settlement. The rich farmland of Wisconsin's south-central plains attracted U.S. and foreign-born people, and the population grew rapidly. Twentieth-century industry led to the rise of many cities along the shores of Lake Michigan, whose waters offered the ability to ship goods to other states and Canada. Most of Wisconsin's population, industry, and farmland is concentrated in the southern half of the state, due to the rougher terrain and climate in the north.

Today the scenic beauty of the northern region makes it a destination for outdoor recreation. The predominance of dairy farms in the south-central agricultural belt has given Wisconsin the nickname of "America's Dairyland," though the state's economy and culture is far more diverse and wide-ranging than this nickname would suggest.

SAY "CHEESE"
Fans of the Green Bay Packers—the professional football team supported and publicly owned by the residents of Green Bay—are called "cheeseheads" because of the hats they wear in homage to the state's prodigious cheese production.

PIONEER VILLAGE
Stonefield Village, a preserved nineteenth-century town, offers a portrait of pioneer life in rural Wisconsin. The mining of lead and other minerals in the 1820s led to a population boom as mining camps turned into bustling towns. American Indian resistance to the loss of land led to the Black Hawk War (1832). The defeated American Indians were then forced onto reservations or pushed farther westward. The settlers included immigrants from Germany, Ireland, and Norway, many of whom farmed wheat and other crops.

CIRCUS PARADE
In the late 1800s, many people lived their whole lives in tiny villages where entertainment was scarce. When circuses traveled to these rural areas by wagon or by train, they were warmly welcomed. Today, Baraboo, Wisconsin is both the 1884 birthplace of the Ringling Brothers circus as well as the home of Circus World Museum, which commemorates the circus's colorful past. Every summer, a circus train wends its way from Baraboo to Milwaukee for a parade and circus, both of which are among the largest in the world.

HARLEY HEAVEN

Milwaukee is the birthplace and headquarters of the world-renowned Harley-Davidson motorcycle company. Meanwhile, dairy farming is conducted throughout the state, which is the top U.S. producer of cheese, butter, and milk.

DID YOU KNOW?

Watertown, Wisconsin, is the site of the nation's first kindergarten. It was established in 1856.

DELLS OF BEAUTY

Along the Wisconsin River in the south-central region of the state are the Wisconsin Dells. The Dells are water-carved canyons with dramatic rock formations. Wisconsin's northern third is a rocky, forested land with high peaks and mineral deposits. The rest of the state consists of gently rolling plains that produce much of the state's large agricultural output.

"FIGHTING BOB"

ROBERT LA FOLLETTE

Politician Robert Marion La Follette served as Wisconsin's governor (1901–1906) and senator (1906–1925) and was a leader of the Progressive movement, which championed the rights and interests of working people and challenged the power of big business. As governor, La Follette instituted many reforms, including government regulation of and higher taxation of railroad companies and direct election by the voting public of state politicians. Many of his reforms were were adopted in other parts of the United States.

La Follette's battles on behalf of the working class earned him the nickname Fighting Bob La Follette.

HOME OF THE BRAT

One-third of Wisconsin's population consisted of immigrants when it achieved statehood. German immigrants brought beer-brewing skills and helped make breweries one of Milwaukee's most important businesses. The state's German heritage is also reflected in its production of bratwurst—known locally as "brats"—and other sausages.

BUSY MILWAUKEE

Milwaukee rose on the lands that the Potawatomi called *Mahn-ah-wauk,* or council grounds. Europeans and Americans began settling the area in the 1830s, and by 1835, the first ship arrived at the new port city, which lay on the shores of Lake Michigan. Today the city is still an active port, as well as a major center of Wisconsin's cultural life.

STATE FACTS

STATE BIRD
Robin

STATE FLOWER
Apple Blossom

STATE TREE
White Pine

CAPITAL
Lansing

POPULATION
9,938,444 (2000)

STATEHOOD
January 26, 1837
Rank: 26th

LARGEST CITIES
Detroit (951,270)
Grand Rapids (197,800)
Warren (138,247)

LAND AREA
56,804 sq. mi.
(147,122 sq. km.)

MICHIGAN

the wolverine state

The name of Lake Michigan, from which the state took its name, is widely attributed to the Algonquian word for "great lake." The Ojibwa of northern Michigan were hunters and fishermen, while the Huron of southern Michigan were farmers, and the Ottawa developed trade routes along the Great Lakes.

In the 1600s, French fur traders established the first European settlements. The region was then populated primarily by fur traders and American Indians until the Erie Canal opened in 1825. The canal connected the Great Lakes and the Midwest to the eastern seaboard. Cheap farmland in southern Michigan drew thousands of settlers.

In the early 1900s, the state became the center of the U.S. automobile industry. Car manufacturing remains economically important in the southern part of the state, chiefly in the cities of Detroit, Dearborn, Flint, and Pontiac. After that, agriculture and mining are the principle industries of the heavily forested north, which is also a popular vacation destination. Miles of Great Lakes shoreline make shipping and transportation a natural part of the state's economy.

The Great Lakes also help create good weather conditions. The water helps to keep temperatures cooler in the summer and milder in the winter, thereby extending the growing season for produce such as cherries, grapes, strawberries, and other fruits grown along the shores of Lake Michigan. Today, Michigan boasts an exceptionally diversified economy in a setting of great natural beauty.

RELIGIOUS MISSION
In 1668, Father Jacques Marquette, a French Jesuit priest, founded a mission and the region's first permanent white settlement at Sault Sainte Marie (pronounced *Soo Saint Marie*).

Porcupine Mountains

WISCONSIN

SHINING LIGHT
The state's extensive coastal areas have longer growing seasons, including, most notably, the strip along Lake Michigan. Proximity to these bodies of water, however, makes for high winds year-round and considerable snowfall in the winter months. Overall, Michigan enjoys warm summers and cold winters, although temperatures vary between the northernmost portion of the state, known as the Upper Peninsula or "UP," and the Lower Peninsula. The "UP" averages 15°F (-9°C) in the winter and 64°F (18°C) in the summer while the more temperate Lower Peninsula has average seasonal temperatures of 26°F (-3°C) and 73°F (23°C).

HITSVILLE, USA
Motown Record Corporation was founded by Berry Gordy Jr. in 1959. The "Motown sound" was a unique mixture of gospel, pop, and rhythm-and-blues that proved enormously popular. It dominated the record charts in the 1960s and early 1970s. Stevie Wonder, The Supremes, and The Jackson 5 all shot to stardom under the Motown label. Today, the original recording studio, Hitsville, USA, stands as part of the Motown Museum.

CRUISING THE COAST

Michigan is made up of two peninsulas that extend into the Great Lakes and are connected by the Mackinac Bridge, which spans the boundary of Lakes Michigan and Huron. The state's extensive coastlines have made it a center of shipping in the Midwest.

Lake Superior

Marquette

CANADA

Sault Sainte Marie

UPPER PENINSULA

•Escanaba

■ *Mackinac Bridge*

LOWER PENINSULA

•Alpena

Lake Huron

•Traverse City

•Roscommon

•Cadillac

MICHIGAN

Saginaw Bay

•Big Rapids

•Bay City

•Saginaw

Lake Michigan

•Flint   Port Huron•

● Grand Rapids

Wyoming•

★ LANSING

•Holland

Windmill Island

Warren•

Battle Creek •Detroit

Kalamazoo•   Ann Arbor•

•Benton Harbor

Monroe•

•Adrian

Lake Erie

INDIANA   OHIO

A FALLS LANDSCAPE

The Lower Peninsula and the eastern portion of the Upper Peninsula consist of central lowlands with plains and gently rolling hills. This region was shaped during its prehistoric past as a lake bottom. The western section of the Upper Peninsula is rocky, forested terrain with many rapids, falls, lakes, and rich mineral deposits. The highest elevations in the state are found in the Huron and Porcupine Mountains in the southwest of the Upper Peninsula.

HIT MAKER

MADONNA

Born in Bay City, entertainer and entrepreneur Madonna Louise Veronica Ciccone, burst onto the music scene in 1983. She scored hit after hit on the pop charts, took the music video to a new artistic level, and started a film career and her own record label. Madonna has become one of the most powerful women in the entertainment industry.

Madonna is also the mother of two children, Lourdes and Rocco.

THE BIRTHPLACE OF THE AUTOMOBILE

In the 1900s, Detroit became the center of the automobile industry. Many of the nation's auto manufacturers remain headquartered in Michigan. Meanwhile, Battle Creek, known as "Cereal City," is home to both Kellogg's and Post, makers of cereal and breakfast foods.

WINDMILL ISLAND

In the 1800s, German, Irish, Finnish, Polish, and Dutch immigrants settled in Michigan and shaped the state's cultural and economic life. The cultivation of tulip bulbs remains an important agricultural product of the town of Holland and its outlying areas, first settled by the Dutch in 1847.

STATE FACTS

STATE BIRD
Eastern Goldfinch

STATE FLOWER
Wild Rose

STATE TREE
Oak

CAPITAL
Des Moines

POPULATION
2,926,324 (2000)

STATEHOOD
December 28, 1846
Rank: 29th

LARGEST CITIES
Des Moines (198,682)
Cedar Rapids (120,758)
Davenport (98,359)

LAND AREA
55,869 sq. mi.
(144,701 sq. km.)

IOWA
the hawkeye state

French explorers Louis Jolliet and Father Jacques Marquette became the first Europeans to reach the Midwest when they canoed down the Mississippi, reaching Iowa on June 25, 1673. Nine years later, Frenchman René-Robert Cavelier, Sieur de La Salle, followed the same path and claimed the region for France. The U.S. took control of Iowa in the Louisiana Purchase in 1803, and officials sent Meriwether Lewis and William Clark to explore it.

Early inhabitants of the Iowa area included the Mound Builders. These people left behind more than 10,000 large dirt mounds filled with tools and weapons; the mounds themselves were used for ceremonial purposes. Later native cultures included the Iowa, Illinois, and Sioux, who lived along the Mississippi River, and the Omaha and Missouri tribes of the western region.

The state was named for the Iowa tribe, who once made the land their home; the word Iowa is believed to mean "beautiful land" in their language. Though the U.S. Army and fur traders established forts in the region, it remained Indian Territory until the 1830s.

Today, Iowa's economy relies on crops grown on its fertile farmland, as well as on revenue from tourist attractions, such as a former Underground Railroad station and the location used in the movie *Field of Dreams*. Residents enjoy the state's glacier-made lakes as well as festivals that celebrate the substantial Danish population that makes up parts of the state.

KEY BORDER RIVERS
Iowa's eastern border is formed by the Mississippi River, along which the state's first towns were built. The Missouri River marks the state's western border. Heavy snowfall fills the rivers and average temperatures range from 18°F to 24°F (-8°C to -4°C) in January and 74°F to 77°F (23°C to 25°C) in July.

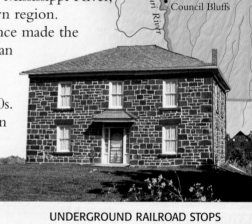

UNDERGROUND RAILROAD STOPS
Hitchcock House in the town of Lewis is one of many Underground Railroad stations throughout the state, which never permitted slavery. The home, owned by Congregation Church Reverend George B. Hitchcock, was a safe haven for runaway slaves and abolitionists.

TWIN ADVICE

ANN LANDERS AND ABIGAIL VAN BUREN

Twin sisters Esther Pauline (Landers) and Pauline Esther (Van Buren) Friedman were born in Sioux City, Iowa, on July 4, 1918. Landers got her name when she took over a *Chicago Sun-Times* advice column called "Ask Ann Landers" in 1955. A year later, her sister began her "Dear Abby" column. The sisters gained attention by writing strong advice on readers's romantic and personal problems, as well as their controversial positions on issues such as the Vietnam War.

The sisters became rivals while writing their internationally published advice columns.

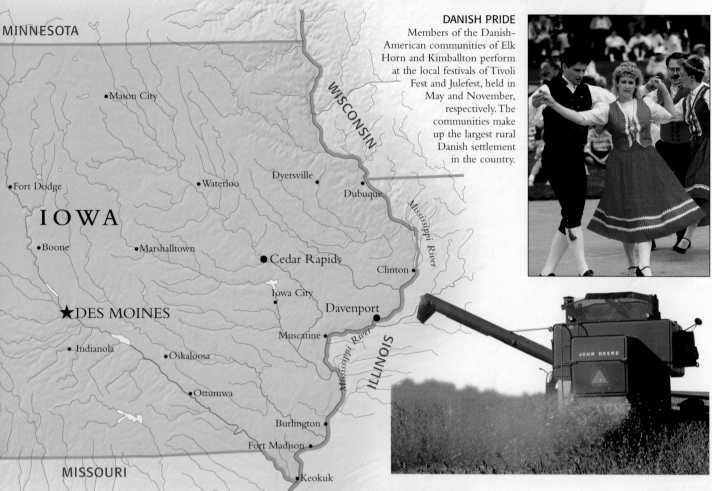

MINNESOTA

• Mason City

• Fort Dodge

IOWA

WISCONSIN

• Waterloo   Dyersville •

Dubuque •

• Boone   • Marshalltown

Mississippi River

⭐ DES MOINES

• Cedar Rapids

Clinton •

Iowa City •

Davenport

• Indianola   • Oskaloosa

Muscatine •

ILLINOIS

Mississippi River

• Ottumwa

Burlington •

Fort Madison •

MISSOURI

• Keokuk

DANISH PRIDE

Members of the Danish-American communities of Elk Horn and Kimballton perform at the local festivals of Tivoli Fest and Julefest, held in May and November, respectively. The communities make up the largest rural Danish settlement in the country.

PROCESSED FOOD PRODUCTION

The largest cereal mill in the nation is a Quaker Oats factory in Cedar Rapids. Iowa's central location in the country's "farm belt" has attracted many food-processing companies. Sioux City has the country's largest popcorn processing plant.

FERTILE SOIL

The deep layers of fertile soil that spread across northern and central Iowa produce some of the country's most valuable soybean yields, used for livestock feed and the production of soybean oil. Corn is another major source of income—the state produces one-fifth of the country's corn supply.

MOVIE MAGIC

The 1989 Oscar-nominated drama *Field of Dreams* was filmed on the grounds of a more than 91-year-old family farm in Dyersville, Iowa, that is now a popular tourist attraction. University of Iowa Writer's Workshop graduate W. P. Kinsella's book, *Shoeless Joe* (1982), was the basis for the movie. Visitors can play ball on the field, which was built in only three days to accommodate filming.

GLACIERS MARK THE LAND

Many of the state's lakes, which freeze in the icy winter climate, were formed millions of years ago from melted glacier deposits. North-central Iowa was flattened by four glaciers that deposited incredibly fertile soil. One glacier moved through northeastern Iowa, leaving behind a hilly region with less productive soil.

STATE FACTS

STATE BIRD
Cardinal

STATE FLOWER
Native Violet

STATE TREE
White Oak

CAPITAL
Springfield

POPULATION
12,419,293 (2000)

STATEHOOD
December 3, 1818
Rank: 21st

LARGEST CITIES
Chicago (2,896,016)
Rockford (150,115)
Aurora (142,990)

LAND AREA
55,584 sq. mi.
(143,963 sq. km.)

ILLINOIS

ILLINOIS

the prairie state

A confederation of Algonquian tribes known as the Illinois, which included the Kickapoo, Ottawa, and Peoria, inhabited the region when French explorers first arrived in the 1670s. Control of the region passed from the French to the British in 1763, and then to the newly formed U.S. Illinois become a state in 1818.

White settlement remained sparse until the era of canal building began in the 1820s, making the state easily accessible to settlers coming from the East in search of farmland. By the eve of the Civil War, Illinois was both the Midwest's commercial and agricultural center, due in part to the growth of Chicago. The fertile prairies of Illinois made it a national leader in the cultivation of corn, as well as the raising of livestock; this remains true today.

With its numerous natural waterways and central location, Illinois has long been a center of transportation and trade, linking the eastern and western United States. First canals, then railroads and roadways, crisscrossed the state, creating a flow of goods and people that have shaped the state and the nation. Illinois's urban centers and stretches of rural farmland, linked by an extensive transportation network, have resulted in a strong, mixed economy. Illinois has always been a center of political and social reform, from its leadership in union organizing in the late 1800s to its 1992 election of Carol Moseley-Braun as the first African-American woman in the U.S. Senate.

DID YOU KNOW?

The Chicago River is dyed green for St. Patrick's Day. The city of Chicago adds 40 pounds (18 kg) of food coloring to the water.

HAYMARKET SQUARE

Illinois in the 1800s was a hotbed of reform, from the fight to end slavery in the 1850s to union organizing in the 1880s and 1890s. In 1886, Chicago's Haymarket Square was the site of a rally: Workers striking for an 8-hour workday were protesting their treatment by police. The rally exploded into violence, leaving seven dead and many more injured. This protest, and others that followed—including the 1894 Pullman railroad strike that also began in Chicago—eventually resulted in major improvements in the lives of working people across the nation.

THE WHOLE HOG

Illinois pork, beef, eggs, and milk make their way to dining tables around the world. Corn, for both human and animal consumption, has long been Illinois's most important cash crop; soybeans and wheat are two others. Illinois's cattle ranches and dairy farms generate about a quarter of the state's agricultural income. Much of the produce is processed in the state as well.

Map labels: IOWA, Mississippi River, Rock Island, Kewanee, Monmouth, Peoria, Macomb, ILLINOIS, Quincy, SPRINGFIELD, Jacksonville, Mississippi River, Edwardsville, East Saint L, Belleville, MISSOURI, Mississippi R

VARIED WEATHER

Illinois's length—385 miles (620 km) from its northernmost point to its southernmost point—makes for a wide range of weather conditions. Northern Illinois is colder and snowier, while the south is warmer and rainier. Average winter temperatures, north and south, range from 22°F to 37°F (-6°C to 3°C); average summer temperatures, north and south, range from 74°F to 80°F (23°C to 27°C), with high humidity. Southern Illinois receives the most rainfall and suffers from flooding. Conversely northern Illinois receives the heaviest snowfall, with up to 38 inches (97 cm) falling in Chicago.

WILDLIFE PRAIRIE PARK

Illinois's landscape was once dominated by the gently rolling grasslands of the Great Prairie. Today this park, near Peoria, preserves pristine grasslands and the animals that live upon it. The rich soil of Illinois's prairie drives the agricultural output of the state.

FARM FUTURES

The Chicago Board of Trade and the Chicago Mercantile Exchange, founded in 1848 and 1898 respectively, rank among the most important futures markets in the world. Futures markets establish the prices of agricultural goods such as wheat, corn, beef, and pork.

SKYSCRAPER BIRTHPLACE

Chicago is considered the birthplace of the skyscraper—the Home Insurance Building, the first such building, was completed there in 1885. The city has since been a center for modern American architecture. With 110 floors and a height of 1,450 feet (442 m), the Sears Tower is the tallest building in North America and a tribute to the industrial might of its home city and state. The building has office space for about 12,000 workers.

ILLINOIS SON

ABRAHAM LINCOLN

Twenty-one-year-old Abraham Lincoln arrived in Illinois in 1830, seeking new opportunities in the fast-growing state. Lincoln became a lawyer and began his political career in the Illinois state legislature before ascending to the U.S. Senate and then to the White House in 1861. As an opponent of slavery, Lincoln's election helped to spark the Civil War. As president, Lincoln freed America's slaves, secured the Union's victory, and worked to heal the nation's wounds. His assassination, shortly after the war ended, left the nation mourning a great leader who promised peace "with malice toward none; with charity for all."

Lincoln served in the Illinois state legislature from 1835 to 1842 before running for U.S. senator.

STATE FACTS

STATE BIRD
Cardinal

STATE FLOWER
Peony

STATE TREE
Tulip Tree

CAPITAL
Indianapolis

POPULATION
6,080,485 (2000)

STATEHOOD
December 11, 1816
Rank: 19th

LARGEST CITIES
Indianapolis (791,926)
Fort Wayne (205,727)
Evansville (121,582)

LAND AREA
35,867 sq. mi.
(92,896 sq. km.)

INDIANA
the hoosier state

Indiana's first inhabitants are believed to be Mound Builders, who developed earthen forts and villages during the first century, A.D. The first European to record observations about the area was René-Robert Cavelier, Sieur de La Salle, in 1679. At that time, American Indians, mostly of the Miami tribe, lived in the state.

More American Indian tribes settled the region throughout the 1700s and 1800s as white settlements along the U.S.'s northeastern seaboard grew and pushed them westward—for this reason the state is called Indiana, or "the land of the Indians." Around 1732, the French founded Indiana's first permanent settlement, Vincennes, and built a fort and fur-trading posts there. Britain eventually gained control of Indiana, but lost the region to the U.S. after the American Revolution.

Americans, including young Abraham Lincoln, began settling the area in the early 1800s. They took advantage of the state's rich farmland, still an asset, and central location in the country. Indiana built its first canal in the 1830s and continues to be an important site for interstate shipping. Today, some of Indiana's waterways, such as the Wabash River, are used to provide hydroelectric power.

The state's residents are called Hoosiers, although the origin of this nickname is unknown. Some say it's because a man named Samuel Hoosier hired workers who came to be called "hoosiers." Others say it's from *hoozer*, Southern slang for "hill." Whatever the nickname's origin, tourists and Hoosiers alike now enjoy the state's landscape of rolling hills, flat plains, and even beaches along Lake Michigan.

LINCOLN'S FIRST HOME
Abraham Lincoln's parents were among the state of Indiana's first white residents. In 1815, they moved from Kentucky to the town that later became known as Santa Claus. A year later they built a one-room log cabin along Pigeon Creek— Lincoln, the 16th president lived there from age 7 to 21. That home, now a national monument, still stands today in what is now Lincoln City. The cabin and the surrounding 200 acres (81 hectares) are part of the Lincoln Boyhood National Memorial. The park also features an 1800 period farm and the burial site of Lincoln's mother, Nancy Hanks Lincoln.

Lake Michigan

Gary • Chesterton • Sou

ILLINOIS

INDIA

Terre Haute

Wabash River

Lincoln City

Ohio River

Pigeon Creek • Evansville

KENTUCKY

MICHIGAN

Wayne

Muncie

OHIO

POLIS

Ohio River

LAKE MICHIGAN SHORELINE

Indiana Dunes State Park in Chesterton stretches three miles (5 km) along Lake Michigan's south shoreline. Along with the beach's enormous sand dunes, visitors can experience the Midwest's most diverse woodlands—1,800 acres (728 hectares) of plants, including white pines and giant wood ferns.

WABASH RIVER

Flowing southwest through Indiana is the 475-mile (764 km) Wabash River. It becomes the state's border with Illinois before emptying into the Ohio River. The Wabash is the largest northern tributary north of the Ohio, and it links with the Tippecanoe and White rivers. Dams on the Wabash control flooding and produce hydroelectricity. The river's main traffic is barges of sand and gravel mined locally. Corn and livestock are raised along the river's fertile basin.

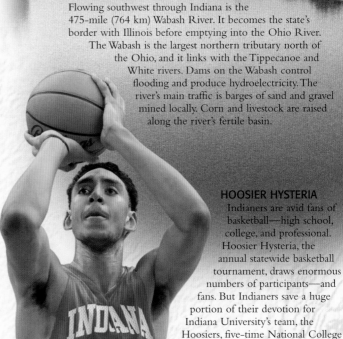

HOOSIER HYSTERIA

Indianers are avid fans of basketball—high school, college, and professional. Hoosier Hysteria, the annual statewide basketball tournament, draws enormous numbers of participants—and fans. But Indianers save a huge portion of their devotion for Indiana University's team, the Hoosiers, five-time National College Athletic Association (NCAA) champs who have appeared in the Final Four a total of thirty-one times. Former players include Isiah Thomas who now coaches the Indiana Pacers.

INDY SPEEDWAY

Each Memorial Day weekend at the Indianapolis Motor Speedway crowds gather to witness the country's most famous car racing event, the Indy 500. The race is part speed and part endurance because the winner must be the leader after 200 laps, or 500 miles (805 km). With an average speed of 160 miles per hour (257 kph), the race takes as many as three hours to complete.

CROSSROADS OF AMERICA

Indiana is called "The Crossroads of America" because its central location is great for interstate shipping, particularly trucking. Indiana has more miles of interstate highway than any other state its size. Four major interstates pass through Indianapolis. The state's 6,600 miles (10,621 km) of railroads also promote trade and carry the state's mining products to other places. Meanwhile, Indiana's broad, fertile plains make it a vital farming state, with corn and soybeans, such as those being grown in the field shown at right, earning half of the state's annual agricultural income.

LATE NIGHT LAUGHTER

DAVID LETTERMAN

Before becoming the host of a national late night TV talk show, David Letterman practiced his craft in and around Indianapolis. Born April 12, 1947, Letterman worked at several radio stations and served as a TV weatherman following his graduation from college. After writing scripts for various sitcoms, Letterman was asked to become a guest host on *The Tonight Show*. He hosted his own show, *Late Night with David Letterman* on NBC before jumping to CBS with *The Late Show with David Letterman* in 1993, where his show still runs today.

David Letterman was the host of a local Indiana children's television show called Clover Power.

STATE FACTS

STATE BIRD
Cardinal

STATE FLOWER
Scarlet Carnation

STATE TREE
Buckeye

CAPITAL
Columbus

POPULATION
11,353,140 (2000)

STATEHOOD
March 1, 1803
Rank: 17th

LARGEST CITIES
Columbus (711,470)
Cleveland (478,403)
Cincinnati (331,285)

LAND AREA
40,948 sq. mi.
(106,055 sq. km.)

OHIO
the buckeye state

By the time European settlers arrived in the region, several tribes, including the Shawnee and Miami, inhabited the land. In 1670, Frenchman René-Robert Cavelier, Sieur de La Salle, became the first European to explore the region. Eighty years later, the British sent Christopher Gist to explore the upper Ohio River Valley. Ohio was actually named after the Iroquois word for "something great," which the tribe used to describe the Ohio River.

After the American Revolution, the region came into U.S. hands as part of the Northwest Territory. On April 7, 1788, the fur-trading Ohio Company founded the first permanent white settlement in Ohio at Marietta. Soon settlers poured into the area to take advantage of its rich soil.

In the early 1800s, Ohio became a trade center thanks to numerous canals built within the state and elsewhere, and due to ports along the shores of Lake Erie, including easy access to the major port of Buffalo, New York. The area was booming by 1869 when the Cincinnati Red Stockings became the first all-professional baseball team, and a year later Benjamin F. Goodrich began manufacturing rubber products in Akron. The state is still a prime area for farming, with both turkey and soybean production being big business. Kids from around the world join in Akron's All-American Soap Box Derby each year, while ski resorts and sites such as Beaver Creek State Park attract tourists of all ages.

GOING PRO
In 1868, the Cincinnati Base Ball Club decided that the only way to produce a truly strong team was to create the nation's first all-professional baseball team. The Cincinnati Red Stockings were born the following year as the first team to play for pay. Their name came from the red socks, or "stockings," that were part of their uniforms.

FIRST ASTRONAUT TO ORBIT EARTH

JOHN GLENN

John Herschel Glenn, Jr., has served his country as a pilot for the U.S. Marines, an astronaut, and a senator. Born in 1921 in Cambridge, Ohio, Glenn grew up in nearby New Concord. In 1942, he left college to serve as a pilot during World War II and the Korean War. An avid flyer, in July 1957 he became the first person to make a nonstop supersonic flight from Los Angeles to New York City. Two years later, NASA chose Glenn to be one of the first astronauts. He flew aboard *Mercury* in February 1962, and became the first person to orbit the planet aboard the capsule *Friendship 7*. In 1974, Glenn was elected as a Democrat from Ohio to the U.S. Senate, where he served four terms. In October 1998, 77-year-old Glenn lifted off aboard the space shuttle *Discovery*, becoming the world's oldest astronaut.

Glenn preparing for his voyage aboard Friendship 7.

ALL-AMERICAN DERBY
The All-American Soapbox Derby, the country's biggest car racing event for kids, has been operating in Ohio since 1934. Begun by Dayton news photographer Myron Scott, a permanent track called Derby Downs was built for the race in Akron two years later. Today, kids from across the world build and race their own cars—commonly made of crates or soapboxes—and compete each August for scholarships, merchandise, and gold jackets in three levels of division races.

MICHIGAN

Tol

Bowling Gre

INDIANA

Springfield •

• Dayton

• Cincinnati

Ohio River

KENTUCKY

CANADA

Lake Erie

● Cleveland

● Elyria

● Warren
Akron ●
Youngstown ●

● Mansfield

● Canton

OHIO

PENNSYLVANIA

ALLEGHENY PLATEAU

★ COLUMBUS

● Cambridge

New
Concord

Ohio River

● Athens

WEST VIRGINIA

Ohio River

● Portsmouth

LAKE ERIE
Ohio's largest body of water
is Lake Erie, the shallowest of
the Great Lakes. It stretches from Toledo
eastward to Buffalo, New York, and lines most of
Ohio's northern border. Ohio also has 44,000 miles
(70,809 km) of rivers and streams, many of which flow
into the lake. Access to these waterways, as well as Ohio's
central location within the country, helped establish it as
one of the nation's manufacturing centers.

ROCK ON
Cleveland became the home of
the Rock and Roll Hall of Fame
and Museum chiefly because local
DJ Alan Freed popularized the phrase
"Rock and Roll" in the city in 1951.
I.M. Pei designed the boldly geometric
building that houses the museum,
intending for it to "mimic the energy of
rock and roll." Each year an international
panel of music experts selects inductees,
who then perform in a nationally
televised award ceremony.

ROCK AND ROLL HALL OF FAME AND MUSEUM
ONE KEY PLAZA

RUBBER—A "GOOD" THING
A worker presses rubber into a tire for race cars
at the Goodyear tire factory in Akron, Ohio.
Goodyear, founded in 1898, was named for
Charles Goodyear, the inventor of vulcanization—
the process of refining rubber for industrial use.
Benjamin F. Goodrich, however, was the person
who opened Ohio's first rubber factory, in 1870.
To start with Goodrich's factory made fire hoses,
but it progressed into tire-making in the 1890s,
when "horseless carriages" became popular.

SNOWY SITES
The Appalachian mountain region in the eastern part of the
state receives approximately 100 inches (254 cm) of
snow a year and has many ski resorts. Average
precipitation for the state is about 38 inches (97
cm), although more rain tends to fall in
southwestern Ohio. In general, Ohio has
cold winters with an average of 28°F
(-2°C) in January. Summers are
warmer and often humid,
with an average July
temperature of 73°F
(23°C).

TOPS IN TURKEYS
As one of the top turkey suppliers in the
nation, Ohio brings in more than $63.5
million in turkey production each year.
Soybeans, however, are Ohio's key farm
product, generating 22 percent of the state's
$5.5 billion agricultural income.

DID YOU KNOW?
James Hoge of Cleveland invented the
first electric traffic lights and installed
them there on August 5, 1914.

STATE FACTS

STATE BIRD
Bluebird

STATE FLOWER
Hawthorn

STATE TREE
Dogwood

CAPITAL
Jefferson City

POPULATION
5,595,211 (2000)

STATEHOOD
August 10, 1821
Rank: 24th

LARGEST CITIES
Kansas City (441,545)
St. Louis (348,189)
Springfield (151,580)

LAND AREA
68,886 sq. mi.
(178,415 sq. km.)

MISSOURI
the show me state

The state of Missouri, and the river that forms its northwest border, take their names from the Missouri tribe that once farmed and hunted in the region's fertile river valleys. In the 1790s, settlers began to flock to the area. They established farms and plantations in southeast Missouri's fertile, swampy land. Missouri became a state in 1821, which provoked one of the first major Congressional debates over slavery in the U.S.

Bounded by mighty rivers that shaped its landscape—the Missouri to the northwest and the Mississippi to the east—these waters also made the state a major departure point for westward-bound settlers in the 1800s. The river ports of St. Louis and Kansas City developed as centers for trade and shipping for both agricultural and industrial goods.

Spring brings rain to the state's many crops; spring is also tornado season. Missouri lies within "Tornado Alley" in the central U.S.

While the origin of the state nickname—the Show Me state—is unknown, central Missouri's diverse, rich urban culture, and the southeast's Ozark Mountains and unique folk culture means that the state has something to show everyone.

BOONE'S LAND
When the U.S. gained possession of Missouri as part of the 1803 Louisiana Purchase, there was already considerable settlement. Daniel Boone, the famed frontiersman, was one of those settlers—his home, now a museum, is shown at left. Missouri first petitioned for statehood in 1818, sparking fierce debates over the balance of slave versus free states. The Missouri Compromise (1820) led to the admission of Missouri as a slave state and the creation of federal guidelines on the issue of slavery in new states.

THE WAY WEST
The Lewis and Clark Expedition set off in 1804 from St. Charles, which lay where the Missouri and Mississippi Rivers converged. That historic journey marked the beginning of Missouri's role as a gateway to westward expansion; several major overland trails began in this region. Today the St. Charles historic district is now part of the city of St. Louis.

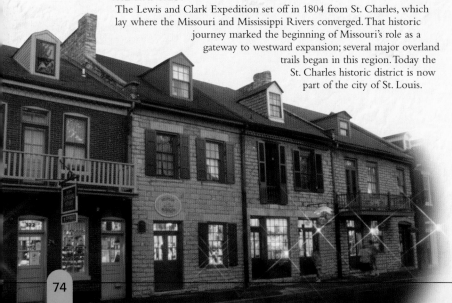

FATHER OF INVENTIONS

GEORGE WASHINGTON CARVER

Born into slavery near Diamond Grove in the early 1860s, George Washington Carver became a teacher and inventor in the agricultural sciences. He helped transform farming practices and the lives of farmers in the American South. In 1896, Carver began teaching and researching at Tuskegee Institute where he pioneered new crops and methods of soil conservation and crop rotation that freed southern farmers from dependence on cotton.

Carver's work gained him international acclaim.

A CHANGEABLE CLIMATE

Long, warm, and humid summers are the rule in Missouri—the average daily temperature in July is 78°F (26°C). Average January temperatures hover around 30°F (-1°C), with moderate snowfall. Missouri's climate is prone to sudden changes, including summertime thunderstorms and brief heatwaves and cold snaps. Missouri is also the site of about of 27 tornadoes per year, given its location in "Tornado Alley." In addition, Missouri's "bootheel" region is also an earthquake zone.

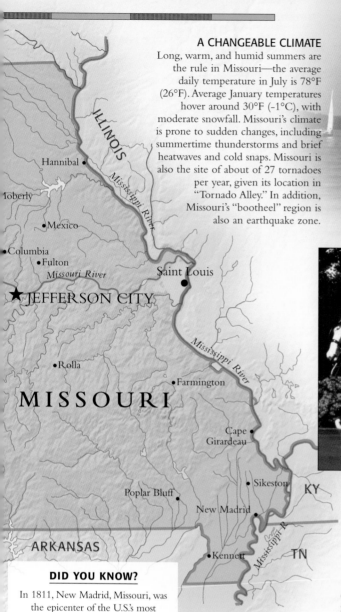

DID YOU KNOW?

In 1811, New Madrid, Missouri, was the epicenter of the U.S.'s most powerful earthquake. It was felt as far as 1,000 miles (1,609 km) away.

BIG BREWERIES

Clydesdales became associated with the Anheuser-Busch brewery in 1933 when a team hauled the first beer brewed in the factory after Prohibition was repealed. The company was founded in 1860 by German immigrant Eberhard Anheuser, who bought a St. Louis brewery that his son-in-law Adolphus Busch turned into one of the nation's most preeminent.

GATEWAY TO THE WEST

St. Louis became known as the "Gateway to the West" in the 1800s, but today the city boasts a diversified manufacturing sector, producing beer and other food products, as well as cars, missiles, and shoes. St. Louis and Kansas City, the state's two largest cities, are home to more than half the state's total population and account for about three-quarters of its industrial activity.

MAKING MUSIC

The invention of the record player in 1877 and the development of radio broadcasting in the 1920s sparked the growth of the recording industry. The Bennie Moten Orchestra was one of the first Kansas City jazz bands to record and popularize the distinctive style developed by the city's vibrant community of jazz musicians. In addition to its important cultural contributions, Kansas City has long served as a center for transportation, shipping, and food processing in the state.

THE PLAINS STATES

American Indian nations such as the Apache and the Dakota (Sioux) first lived, farmed, and hunted on the Great Plains—vast, rolling, grass-covered prairies with few trees. The Lewis and Clark Expedition was the first to map the region; they were sent to explore this newly acquired U.S. territory by President Thomas Jefferson in 1804. Railroad construction in the 1860s sparked a population boom. Available land, and the ease of railroad travel—as compared to traveling across the country on foot and by wagon—brought thousands of settlers to the region.

The railroad dramatically increased white settlement. This changed life for the region's American Indian population, and for its wildlife population, too.

In the 1870s, gold was discovered in South Dakota's Black Hills, attracting thousands more fortune-seekers. The increasing white population caused intense conflicts with American Indians, who eventually lost control of their territory to the U.S. government. By 1889, "Indian Territory," which once stretched across the entire Plains, covered only half of Oklahoma. The region's fertile soil and extensive grasslands, ideal for farming as well as grazing livestock, had given these settlers reason to put down roots.

LANDSCAPE

The enormous plains provided the region with its name, but the area also encompasses tremendous geological diversity. A network of rivers—including the Missouri, the Arkansas, and the Kansas—provide transportation and recreation. North and South

Map

NORTH DAKOTA
★ Bismarck

SOUTH DAKOTA
Pierre ★
■ BADLANDS
Mount Rushmore
Missouri
Crazy Horse Monument
SAND HILLS

NEBRASKA
Lincoln ★

Topeka ★
Kansas River
KANSAS

Arkansas River

Oklahoma City ★
OKLAHOMA

Corn and wheat are among the region's top agricultural products. Nebraska produces the most corn of any Plains state, with more than 8,500 acres (3,440 hectares) planted.

The hunting of the buffalo that once roamed the plains, was central to the lives of Plains Indians, whether they lived a nomadic lifestyle or practiced farming in permanent villages.

KEY DATES

1803 The United States acquires much of the Great Plains region from France as part of the Louisiana Purchase.

1854 A five-year conflict between pro- and antislavery settlers breaks out in Kansas, which people began calling "Bleeding Kansas."

1862 The Homestead Act grants free land to settlers who will farm it for five years. The act spurs settlement of Nebraska and, later, North Dakota.

Dakota's Badlands—so named because of their harsh landscape—were slowly sculpted over thousands of years by constant water erosion. An ancient sea in the center of the continent once covered the Plains. It receded about 85 million years ago, leaving behind fertile soil. The Plains region also includes mountains in southern Oklahoma, the Sand Hills of central Nebraska—sand dunes held in place by their grassy covering—and the prairie grasslands of northeastern Kansas.

Kansas, Nebraska, and Oklahoma lie in a region known as "Tornado Alley," which experiences the heaviest concentration of tornadoes in the world.

CLIMATE

Spring in the Plains states brings the rain needed to cultivate crops that play a central role in the region's economy. Spring is also tornado season, which continues into summer. The Plains states lie within "Tornado Alley," a region known for its high incidence of these fierce storms. Meanwhile, summer temperatures can reach more than 100°F (38°C). Drought is not uncommon in these areas.

Fall is harvest time, and conditions are generally temperate throughout the region. With the onset of winter, temperatures can sink well below 0°F (-18°C). Southern Kansas receives an average of about 1 foot (.3 m) of snow each winter, west-central Kansas about 18 inches (46 cm), and northwest Kansas about 2 feet (.6 m). Heavy winds can result in blizzard conditions.

LIFESTYLE

The region has few professional sports teams, but Plains states residents have found plenty to cheer about. Champion college football teams such as the University of Nebraska Huskers and the Oklahoma State Sooners draw huge crowds. Meanwhile, others have made art

The University of Nebraska Huskers—named for their native state's leading agricultural product, corn—attract enthusiastic fans.

from the natural world. South Dakota is home to two enormous sculptures—Mt. Rushmore and a monument to Crazy Horse, an Oglala Sioux warrior. Meanwhile, Kansas artist Stan Herd exemplifies the region's spirit, with his "earth art," constructed in fields with crops, plants, soil, and rocks.

ECONOMY

Agriculture is central to the economic well-being of the region, with its vast fields of crops and grazing land for cattle and sheep. Wheat, corn, and livestock are only some of the important farm goods produced and shipped around the world. Processing the crops into foodstuffs—such as milling wheat into flour—provides employment for many Plains staters.

The region also has factories that manufacture such goods as paper products and airplanes. An abundance of mineral deposits has made mining the livelihood of many. Oil, petroleum, coal, and natural gas deposits all continue to fuel the economy of the Plains states.

1893 American Indians lose much of their territory in Oklahoma. They are forced onto reservations, to allow further white settlement.

1931 Severe droughts combined with poor farming lead to an estimated loss of 850,000,000 tons of topsoil. The drought does not end until the fall of 1939.

1941 Mt. Rushmore is completed—fourteen years after the sculpture was begun. The nose of each president is approximately 18 feet (5 m) long.

1954 The Supreme Court deems segregation unconstitutional in the landmark case *Brown v. Board of Education,* filed three years earlier in Topeka, Kansas.

STATE BIRD
Western Meadowlark

STATE FLOWER
Wild Prairie Rose

STATE TREE
American Elm

CAPITAL
Bismarck

POPULATION
634,448 (2000)

STATEHOOD
November 2, 1889
Rank: 39th

LARGEST CITIES
Fargo (90,599)
Bismarck (55,532)
Grand Forks (49,321)

AREA
68,976 sq. mi.
(178,648 sq. km.)

NORTH DAKOTA
the peace garden state

MAJOR MANUFACTURING
In 1947, the Bobcat Company formed to provide local farmers with the machinery they needed. Today the company has its headquarters in Fargo and is an international supplier of industrial machines.

Various American Indian cultures made North Dakota home as many as 10,000 years ago. By the 1700s, the Mandan, Hidatsa, and Akikara lived in farming villages along the Missouri River. The tribes of the Dakota (Sioux) Nation, from which the state derives its name, hunted bison on the plains.

The French claimed the region in 1682, but conflict over the land raged among the British, French, Spanish, and American Indians for over a century until the newly formed United States gained control of the region after the 1803 Louisiana Purchase. It wasn't until the railroads reached the region in the 1870s that white settlers came to the area in great numbers. After that, farms and cattle ranches sprang up.

North Dakota's treeless prairies are still home to vast stretches of cattle pasture and wheat fields—relatively few large towns and cities can be found. Hot, dry summers provide a long growing season; the winds that whip across the plains make for cooler and more comfortable summertime temperatures in the evenings, but can also lead to dust storms. North Dakota winters are long and cold, with average January temperatures in Bismarck of 9°F (-13°C).

FRONTIER FORT
From 1804 to 1806, Captain Meriwether Lewis and Lieutenant William Clark led an expedition to explore the vast territory west of the Mississippi River. Their camp, near present-day Bismarck, was called Fort Mandan. Here they gathered critical information and supplies.

MONTANA

• Williston

Lake Sakat

Dickinson •

BADLANDS

BADLANDS AND MORE
In the southwest, wind and water deeply eroded the region's soft soil, which lacks ground cover, to create the spectacular jagged hills and deep gullies of the Badlands. French-Canadian fur trappers first gave the region its name because this foreboding terrain was difficult or "bad" land to travel across. Not all of North Dakota is bad land—there are prairies and mountains as well.

PLAINS SOD HOUSE
Congress passed the Homestead Act in 1862, which granted 160 acres (65 ha) of federal land free to those willing to live and farm on it for five years. Farmers and ranchers flocked to the region. Trees were scarce, and without a ready supply of wood, settlers used the earth itself to build their homes. The grassy earth, called sod, was cut into bricks that were stacked to form houses and barns. These earthen houses were cool in summer and warm in winter.

MIGHTY MISSILES

Farmers and ranchers have long appreciated North Dakota's wide-open spaces, but more recently, the state has become home to many federal air bases and missile sites. These military installations have made the federal government an important employer in the state. The 65,000-pound (29,484-kg) Minuteman missile requires a concrete silo built 80 feet (24 m) deep into the ground.

A PARK FOR PEACE

In 1932, the International Peace Garden was established along the U.S.-Canadian border. The gardens commemorates the longtime peaceful coexistence of the two countries, which share the longest undefended border in the world. Located in the Turtle Mountains, the garden is surrounded in the north by the forest preserves of Manitoba, a Canadian province, and the wheat fields of North Dakota's prairies to the south.

DID YOU KNOW?

The first clothes dryer was invented in 1930 in Devil's Lake by Ross Moore, who didn't want his mother to have to hang laundry to dry during North Dakota's long, cold winters.

CANADA

• Minot

Devil's Lake

Grand Forks

MINNESOTA
Red River of the North

NORTH DAKOTA

Missouri River

Mandan •   ★

West Fargo •
• Jamestown   Fargo •

BISMARCK

Lake Oahe

SOUTH DAKOTA

WAVING WHEAT

Farming and ranching on the prairies has long been North Dakota's major source of income. Today, wheat and livestock remain the two leading farm products. Sunflowers, barley, and potatoes are just some of the other crops raised on the state's vast tracts of farmland. The processing of farm goods into food products, such as flour, is also one of the state's chief industries.

SURVEYING THE RANGE

The railroads arrived in North Dakota in the 1870s and provided ranchers with a means to transport the beef they raised to markets outside the state. In the 1880s, drought, followed by fierce winter weather, ended open-range grazing and led to smaller, fenced-in cattle ranches. Today hogs and beef and dairy cattle are raised in the state and continue to fuel its economy.

WESTWARD LEADER

SACAGAWEA

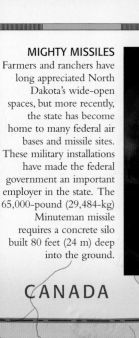

Sacagawea was born about 1787 into a Shoshone tribe in Idaho. She was captured by the Hidatsa in about 1800 and taken to live with them along the shores of the Missouri River in North Dakota. There she became the wife of a French-Canadian trapper. The Lewis and Clark Expedition entered the Hidatsa's winter camp at Fort Mandan, and when the explorers left the fort in April 1805, Sacagawea, her husband, and their infant son Jean-Baptiste joined their party. Sacagawea's skills as guide, interpreter, woodswoman, and emissary to the American Indians they encountered—all while she cared for her newborn baby on the difficult journey—helped insure the party's survival and have made her an American legend.

A likeness of Sacagawea appears on the dollar coin, introduced in 1999.

STATE FACTS

STATE BIRD
Ringed-neck Pheasant

STATE FLOWER
Pasqueflower

STATE TREE
Black Hills Spruce

CAPITAL
Pierre

POPULATION
754,844 (2000)

STATEHOOD
November 2, 1889
Rank: 40th

LARGEST CITIES
Sioux Falls (123,975)
Rapid City (59,607)
Aberdeen (24,658)

LAND AREA
75,885 sq. mi.
(196,524 sq. km.)

SOUTH DAKOTA
the coyote state

South Dakota was named for the confederation of American Indians who had occupied the region for more than 300 years. As part of the Louisiana Purchase, the region was mapped by the Lewis and Clark Expedition and supported a vibrant fur trading community. In the 1868 Treaty of Fort Laramie, the federal government ceded control of the region west of the Missouri River to the Dakota, or Sioux, Nation. The 1870s gold rush in the Black Hills led to increased settlement by whites and the inevitable loss of land for the American Indians.

On November 2, 1889, South Dakota was granted statehood. Farming, ranching, and food processing have always been staples of the state economy, with manufacturing and tourism becoming more important in the last few decades. The drier climate and grass-covered plains of western South Dakota are best suited to ranching.

Visitors come to this region to enjoy its wide-open spaces and magnificent topography. The Black Hills of South Dakota are home to Mount Rushmore; these hills also honor the state's American Indian heritage with a 563-foot- (172-m-) high sculpture of Crazy Horse, an Oglala Sioux leader who led resistance against white settlement of the region until his untimely death in 1877.

DID YOU KNOW?
The nose of each of the presidents carved into Mount Rushmore is approximately 20 feet (6 m) long. From chin to forehead, the heads measure 60 feet (18 m) in all.

CRAZY HORSE
It was 1939 when the Lakota Sioux first invited sculptor Henry Korczak to carve a memorial to the American Indian leader Crazy Horse, who died while a prisoner of the U.S. Army. Korczak created a model of the planned monument (above left), and work began in 1948. The monument, to be carved into the cliff face (above right), is still in progress.

WOUNDED KNEE
Lieutenant Sydney Cloman went to Wounded Knee, South Dakota, to draw an official map of the battleground. Wounded Knee, the final armed battle between American Indians and the U.S. Army, took place there in 1890. 300 Lakota Sioux were slaughtered. Among the U.S. Army troops were survivors of the Battle of Little Big Horn. The federal government at that time feared that American Indians were going to fight against being removed from their land and forced onto reservations.

NORTH DAKOTA

TH DAKOTA

Lake Oahe

★PIERRE

Missouri River

Aberdeen

Watertown

Huron

Brookings

MINNESOTA

Mitchell

Sioux Falls

Great Plains

Yankton

NEBRASKA

Vermillion

THE REAL WIZARD OF OZ

L. FRANK BAUM

Writer and journalist L. Frank Baum was among those who went to South Dakota in the 1880s searching for greater economic opportunity. Baum arrived in Aberdeen in 1888 where he worked as a storekeeper and then as a reporter. In 1900, Baum published *The Wonderful Wizard of Oz*, the first in a best-selling series of children's books about the fantastical Land of Oz.

The 1939 film, The Wizard of Oz, is based on Baum's novels.

CORN PALACE

Mitchell, in southeastern South Dakota, is home to the Corn Palace. First built in 1892, this structure pays homage to the state's agricultural riches with exterior murals re-created yearly from corn, wheat, oats, and other native crops. Used today for shows, sports competitions, and other events, the Corn Palace highlights the importance of farming to the state's economy.

STAKING A CLAIM

Melted gold is poured into an ingot mold. Although the Homestake Mine is no longer active, it was once the world's largest. From 1877 to 1901, more than $100 million in gold was extracted from the Homestake Mine alone.

COMPUTERS IN COWLAND

Farming and ranching remain the backbone of South Dakota's economy but manufacturing has grown in importance. Gateway was founded in 1985 in an Iowa farmhouse by South Dakota native Ted Waitt, and today is heaquartered in South Dakota. The company is one of the nation's top producers of personal computers. Gateway's unique cow-spotted boxes reflect its origins in America's heartland.

MOUNT RUSHMORE

The Mount Rushmore National Memorial is carved into the bluffs of the Black Hills. The heads of four U.S. presidents—George Washington, Thomas Jefferson, Theodore Roosevelt, and Abraham Lincoln—are each about 60 feet (18 m) high. American sculptor Gutzon Borglum began work on the memorial in 1927 and it was completed in 1941.

WINDY PLAINS

South Dakota's weather tends to be extreme with hot summers and cold, snowy winters. Severe thunderstorms are common in the spring and summer months in the state's center, although summer droughts are also a concern in central and western sections of the state. January temperatures average as low as 18°F (-7°C) while July averages 72°F (22°C).

NEBRASKA
the cornhusker state

Nebraska's name was derived from the Oto word for the Platte River, which flows through the middle of the state. The region was home to many American Indian cultures including the Omaha, Oto, Pawnee, Cheyenne, and Comanche. Spanish and French fur traders were the first Europeans to enter the area—they plied their trade during the 1700s as their leaders vied for control of the territory.

The U.S. government gained sole possession of the area in 1803 and it became an important gateway to points further west during the mid- to late-1800s. With the passage of the Homestead Act in 1862, and construction of the first transcontinental railroad, settlement of Nebraska by white people developed rapidly.

By 1890, Nebraska's population numbered nearly one million, including many immigrants from Germany and other northern European nations. The cultivation of livestock and corn on the state's farms and ranches drove the state's economy in its earliest years and continues to do so today. Nebraska is also headquarters for many insurance companies, just one of many businesses that have helped to diversify the state's economy. The relatively flat and treeless land found in much of the state contributes to dramatic weather patterns such as severe thunderstorms, hailstorms, tornadoes, and blizzards—common occurrences across the state.

CHIMNEY ROCK

This 445-foot- (136-km-) tall rock formation was a landmark for the nearly half million settlers who traveled west on the Oregon Trail in the second half of the 1800s. Nebraska's landscape is not just semi-arid plains. The treeless, rolling grasslands of the Sand Hills cover much of northern Nebraska, while prairie land is found in the east. The river valleys of the Missouri and Platte Rivers offer lush landscape with fertile soil for farming.

THE RANCHING WAY

This prosperous cattle ranch, in Custer County, Nebraska, was established in the late 1800s. White settlers were drawn to Nebraska's abundant pastures and farmland. Cattle ranches still predominate in northwest and north-central Nebraska, and agriculture remains important to the state's economy. Corn is the chief crop, with meatpacking, flour milling, and vegetable canning ranking among the state's leading industries.

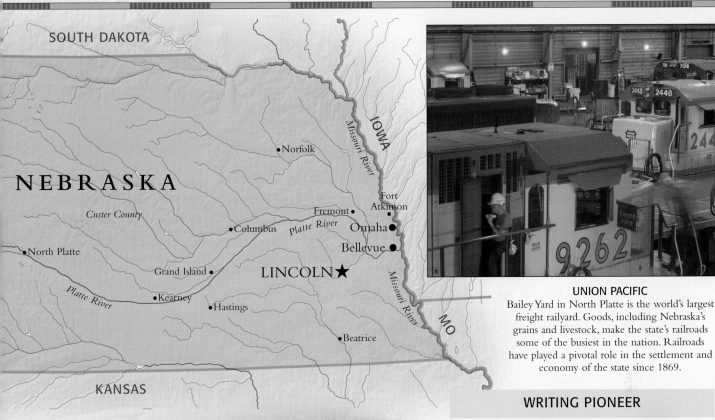

SOUTH DAKOTA

NEBRASKA

IOWA

Missouri River

Custer County

•Norfolk

Fort
Atkinson

Fremont•
•Columbus   Platte River   Omaha•
•North Platte   Bellevue•

Grand Island •
                 LINCOLN ★
Platte River   •Kearney
                •Hastings

MO

Missouri River

•Beatrice

KANSAS

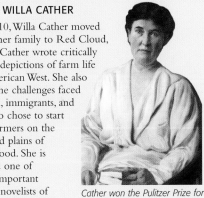

UNION PACIFIC

Bailey Yard in North Platte is the world's largest freight railyard. Goods, including Nebraska's grains and livestock, make the state's railroads some of the busiest in the nation. Railroads have played a pivotal role in the settlement and economy of the state since 1869.

WRITING PIONEER

WILLA CATHER

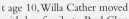

At age 10, Willa Cather moved with her family to Red Cloud, Nebraska. Cather wrote critically acclaimed depictions of farm life in the American West. She also wrote of the challenges faced by women, immigrants, and others who chose to start anew as farmers on the prairies and plains of her childhood. She is considered one of the most important American novelists of the twentieth century.

Cather won the Pulitzer Prize for her novel One of Ours *(1922).*

CARHENGE

Travelers on western Nebraska's Highway 87 are treated to the sight of Carhenge. Carhenge is a replica of Stonehenge—England's famous prehistoric site of monumental standing stones—but it's made of vintage American cars. The brainchild of Nebraska artist and native Jim Reinders, Carhenge includes other examples of "car art" and attracts visitors from around the world.

DID YOU KNOW?

In 1927, Edwin Perkins invented Kool-Aid in Hastings, Nebraska. Hastings created a powdered drink mix when the bottled beverage he invented proved too heavy to ship.

LIGHTNING ON THE RANGE

Severe thunderstorms often roll across Nebraska's prairies and plains in spring and summer, the seasons with the highest levels of precipitation. Tornadoes are also common during these months. Blizzard conditions, with high winds and heavy snowfall, are common in the winter months, with average January temperatures ranging from 20°F to 29°F (-7°C to -2°C) across the state.

FORT ATKINSON

The U.S. Army established this fort to regulate the growing fur trade and resolve disputes between white settlers and American Indians. The fort also served as a departure point for explorers and settlers headed further west. Nebraska's first farm, school, library, hospital, and sawmill were also part of this fort.

KANSAS

the sunflower state

STATE FACTS

STATE BIRD
Western Meadowlark

STATE FLOWER
Native Sunflower

STATE TREE
Cottonwood

CAPITAL
Topeka

POPULATION
2,688,418 (2000)

STATEHOOD
January 29, 1861
Rank: 34th

LARGEST CITIES
Wichita (344,284)
Overland Park (149,080)
Kansas City (146,866)

LAND AREA
81,815 sq. mi
(211,901 sq. km)

The Plains Indians, among them the Witchita and the Kansa, lived on Kansas's Great Plains. They hunted the huge herds of bison, or buffalo, that roamed the middle of the North American continent. It was the Kansa people who gave the state its name—the word means "people of the south wind."

The flat grasslands of the Great Plains cover central and western Kansas, providing good grazing and farmland. The eastern portion of the state has rolling hills and valleys and receives the most precipitation, while the plains region receives much less and can suffer from drought conditions. White settlers didn't arrive until 1827, when wagon trains began moving west along the Santa Fe Trail. By the end of the Civil War, however, railroads helped make Kansas a center of the cattle industry. Kansas "cow towns" sprang up at rail depots, where cattle were put onto stock cars bound for the slaughterhouses of the Midwest.

Frontier marshals such as Wyatt Earp also came to Kansas to bring law and order to the ungoverned region, and to make their own fortunes. Today Kansas's cattle ranches are still leaders in the production of livestock. And, with its abundant and fertile soil, Kansas boasts an agricultural output that has continued to justify its reputation as "America's Breadbasket."

ANCIENT SEAS
A vast prehistoric sea once covered all of Kansas. It receded more than 85 million years ago, leaving a wealth of fossils behind. Kansas's geologic past also provides rich deposits of today's building blocks, including clay, petroleum, chalk, and sand.

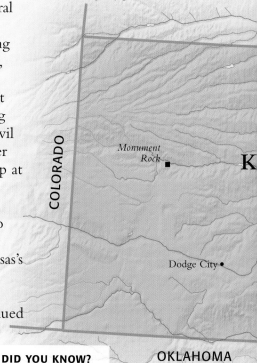

COLORADO

Monument Rock ■

K

Dodge City ●

OKLAHOMA

DODGE CITY
Railroads connected Texas ranchland to big cities, passing through Kansas along the way. As a result, Kansas frontier towns became important marketplaces for cattle being transported by rail. The fortunes to be gained in the cattle business sometimes led to lawlessness and disorder. Today Dodge City remains a symbol of America's romantic vision of the "Wild West."

DID YOU KNOW?
Charles Curtis of Kansas is the only American Indian to have served as a U.S. vice president (1929–1933).

BISON IN WINTER
A shaggy bison, such as those immortalized in Kansas's state song "Home on the Range," is shown weathering a Kansas winter. Temperatures average 30°F (-1°C) in January and 79°F (26°C) in the July. On average, Kansas receives 27 inches (69 cm) of snow each year, but the eastern prairies can receive up to 40 inches (102 cm), with the western plains receiving an average of 17 inches (43 cm). Kansas also averages 47 tornadoes each year.

CROP ART

A Kansas native and artist, Stan Herd sculpts artwork from crops, stones, and other natural materials. These massive "earth works" are best viewed from the air—they can cover several acres (hectares). At left, Herd has commemorated Kansas daughter and aviation pioneer Amelia Earhart in a Kansas field.

FROM FARM...

Kansas's economy is a combination of both agriculture and industry. The state's growing season is long—crops can be cultivated from April through September, helping Kansas meet the nation's need for grain, beef, and other agricultural products, including the seeds from sunflowers, the state flower. Today Kansas is a national leader in grain storage and milling wheat into flour, as well as the processing of its other crops into food goods, including sunflower oil.

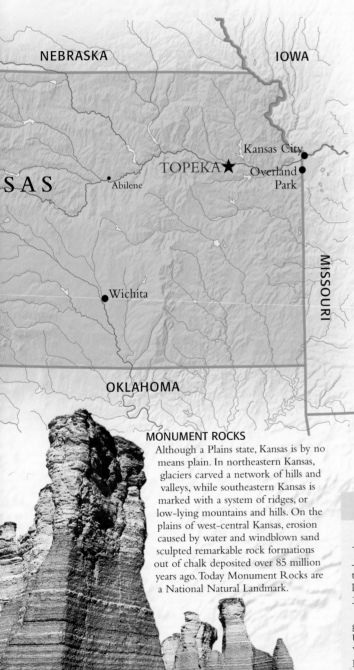

MONUMENT ROCKS

Although a Plains state, Kansas is by no means plain. In northeastern Kansas, glaciers carved a network of hills and valleys, while southeastern Kansas is marked with a system of ridges, or low-lying mountains and hills. On the plains of west-central Kansas, erosion caused by water and windblown sand sculpted remarkable rock formations out of chalk deposited over 85 million years ago. Today Monument Rocks are a National Natural Landmark.

...TO FACTORY

Since World War II, Kansas's manufacturing sector has boomed, and now provides a wide range of goods, from snowmobiles to dishwashers. Cessna, the nation's largest manufacturer of private planes, is located in Wichita, Kansas. The state has long been among the top airplane-manufacturers in the nation, producing as much as 60 percent of general use aircraft.

KANSAS LIKES IKE

DWIGHT D. EISENHOWER

Eisenhower was raised and schooled in Abilene, Kansas, which today is the site of the Eisenhower Center—a library and museum dedicated to the 34th president.

Eisenhower became a five-star general in the U.S. Army. He helped lead U.S. and Allied troops to victory in World War II. A military hero, Eisenhower was later elected president in 1952. During his two terms, Eisenhower brought an end to the Korean War and worked to end the segregation of black and white Americans.

"I like Ike" was Eisenhower's presidential campaign slogan.

STATE FACTS

STATE BIRD
Scissor-tailed Flycatcher

STATE FLOWER
Mistletoe

STATE TREE
Redbud

CAPITAL
Oklahoma City

POPULATION
3,450,654 (2000)

STATEHOOD
November 16, 1907
Rank: 46th

LARGEST CITIES
Oklahoma City (506,132)
Tulsa (393,049)
Norman (95,694)

LAND AREA
68,667 sq. mi
(177,848 sq. km.)

OKLAHOMA
the sooner state

NM

TEXAS

Oklahoma's diverse landscape includes arid high plains in the west, lush river valleys in the center, and forested hills and mountains to the east and south. The state's tourist trade thrives on its many significant American Indian historic sites, outdoor recreation on its mountains and man-made lakes, a plethora of rodeos and horse shows, and much more.

The Choctaw words *okla,* meaning "people," and *humma,* meaning "red," were combined to create the state's name. The U.S. took over the region in 1803; it was then home to the Comanche, Witchita, and others. Decades later, a desire for more land led the government to force Cherokee, Creek, and other native peoples from their homelands in the eastern U.S. to journey to "Indian Territory." Created in 1834, the territory originally included most of Oklahoma, as well as parts of Kansas and Nebraska.

Oklahoma became known as the Sooner State when the government opened up the land to white settlement. On April 22, 1889, settlers rushed to claim 160 acres (65 hectares) of free land. But some settlers snuck in beforehand and were called "sooners." The region's newest residents became farmers and ranchers. In the 1930s, however, poor farming practices and drought led to major dust storms in the state's western high plains. An Associated Press correspondent reporting from Guyman, Oklahoma called the area a "Dust Bowl." Farms were destroyed and thousands of farming families were forced to seek their fortunes elsewhere. Conservation efforts eventually restored Oklahoma's soil. Today, farming, cattle ranching, and oil are important to the state's economy.

DID YOU KNOW?
The first automatic parking meter was installed in Oklahoma City in 1935. It was invented by Oklahoma resident Carlton Cole Magee.

DREAMS TURNED TO DUST
In the 1930s, several years of drought led to massive dust storms, which lifted up the loose topsoil and blew it off the cropland. Many farms, such as this one, were abandoned—the farmyards and buildings became filled with dry, drifting earth. The livelihoods of thousands of Oklahoma farmers were destroyed; many left the state and headed to California and elsewhere, hoping to escape grinding poverty. It took 40 years for the state's population to be restored to pre-Dust Bowl levels.

THIS LAND WAS HIS LAND

WOODY GUTHRIE

Born in Okemah, Oklahoma in 1912, singer and composer Woody Guthrie witnessed the devastation of the Dust Bowl firsthand—it destroyed his family's farm. A teen during the Great Depression, Guthrie traveled the nation by rail, living and working among the rural and urban poor. Their lives became the subjects of some of his most important songs, including "Tom Joad," a chronicle of the lives of victims of the Dust Bowl. The social commentary on America's dispossessed in Guthrie's work influenced Bob Dylan and an entire generation of younger American musicians.

Guthrie's best-known—and best-loved—song is "This Land Was Made for You and Me."

KANSAS

MISSOURI

Miami

• Woodward

• Ponca City

• Bartlesville

• Stillwater   Tulsa

• Clarmore

OKLAHOMA

• Muskogee

El Reno •   ★ OKLAHOMA CITY

Norman •   Shawnee •   • Okemah

• Chickasha

ARKANSAS

• McAlester

• Ada

• Altus   Duncan •   Arbuckle Mountains

Red River   • Ardmore

TEXAS   • Durant

A SCENIC LAND
Turner Falls Park in the Arbuckle Mountains features a 77-foot (23 m) waterfall in the midst of lush, forested hills—a perfect summer spot. Oklahomans generally enjoy long, hot summers and short, relatively mild winters.

RED EARTH FESTIVAL
The Red Earth Native American Cultural Festival, held every June in Oklahoma City, preserves and promotes American Indian culture, crafts, and artists from throughout North America, making it one of the largest events of its kind. Many participants, such as this boy, dress in traditional ceremonial clothing. American Indians have called Oklahoma home for 15,000 years, and the state's rich Indian heritage is celebrated all over.

IN MEMORIUM
Much of the Alfred P. Murrah Federal Building in Oklahoma City was destroyed April 19, 1995 in an explosion that killed 149 adults and 19 children and injured more than 500. Timothy McVeigh was convicted of planting the bomb. In 1997 the Oklahoma City National Memorial was established on the site, with a memorial, an institute dedicated to stopping terrorism, and a museum.

COWBOY CULTURE
Oklahoma City became a center of trade and transport for the state's cattle industry in the 1890s. Its Stockyards City remains one of the nation's largest cattle markets. Oklahoma celebrates its cowboy heritage with the National Cowboy and Western Heritage Museum in the state capital. The state also hosts the International Finals Rodeo (at right), as well as many other horse shows and rodeos.

BLACK GOLD
Since the 1890s, abundant oil fields throughout the state have generated much state income; the discovery of oil in Oklahoma City in 1928 led to the drilling of many wells in the city itself, making Oklahoma the only state with an oil well under its capitol building!

THE SOUTHWEST STATES

About 1,000 years ago, the Navajo migrated from Canada and settled in Arizona and New Mexico. Their culture and lifestyle was strongly influenced by the Pueblo peoples already living in the region. Spanish explorers first entered the area in 1528, and claimed it for Spain in 1537. Spanish missions, or churches, were established in the late 1600s in territories that became Texas, New Mexico, and Arizona, but substantial settlement by whites did not take root for another century. When Mexico gained its independence from Spain in 1821, the region came under Mexican control.

The Native Americans of the Southwest produce some of the most distinctive arts and crafts in the nation, such as this the Navajo pot. Pottery, rugs, and jewelry are among the artifacts that help nurture and sustain Native ways of life.

Spanish vaqueros, or cowboys, taught the tricks of their trade to settlers in Texas in the 1820s. The era of the cowboy on the open ranges of the Southwest lasted until the 1890s, when ranches were fenced in.

Waves of U.S. settlement, including cotton farms on the Texas plains, led to the Texas Revolution and the creation of the independent republic of Texas in 1836. The U.S. annexed Texas and made it a state in 1845, which sparked the Mexican-American War. When this conflict ended, the U.S. had control of the Southwest states. Hispanic culture has had a tremendous impact on life in the Southwest; its influence can be seen in the area's language and religion, as well as its architecture, food, and dance. The border with Mexico ensures a constant exchange of goods that drives this region's economy.

CLIMATE

Less than five inches (13 cm) of rain falls per year in the arid desert climate of much of the Southwest, which offers sunny, clear skies year-round. Snowfall is common in the Southwest's mountains; up to 300 inches (762 cm) of snow falls per year in New Mexico's mountains. With the Sierra Nevadas to the west preventing moist air from reaching the state, Nevada is the nation's driest state, with less than 9 inches (23 cm) of rain or snow falling each year. Water is a valuable and scarce resource throughout much of the region; the Hoover Dam on the Colorado River at the Nevada-Arizona border is one of many water redistribution projects in the

KEY DATES

1537 Explorer Francisco Vasquez de Coronado claims the Southwest for Spain.

1835 The Texas Revolution begins. In 1836, U.S. settlers defeat the Mexican Army at the Battle of San Jacinto and form the Republic of Texas.

1859 Silver is discovered at the Comstock Lode in Nevada. Virginia City is established.

Southwest. Northern Nevada has the region's coldest climate, with an average January temperature of 24°F (-4°C), while 34 °F (1°C) is January's average in New Mexico.

LIFESTYLE

Virginia City, Nevada, was one of many Southwest mining boom towns that grew up seemingly overnight in the second half of the 1800s. Today, the silver deposits are depleted, but along with many other towns like it, Virginia City has developed into a tourist attraction that preserves the history of the Southwest. The red rock valley of the Grand Canyon is the most famous of the region's natural wonders, which range from the Saguaro cactus of Arizona's deserts, to the lush valleys of the Rio Grande, which flows through New Mexico and forms the Texas-Mexico border. The region's diversity of peoples is shown in the Mexican and American Indian arts and crafts available throughout the area; delicate Mexican jewelry and brightly painted Pueblo pottery fill the markets.

A crescent moon hangs over a saguaro and an ocotillo cactus at Kofa National Wildlife Refuge.

Desert covers much of New Mexico and Arizona; the 665,400-acre (269,287-hectare) Kofa National Wildlife Refuge in Arizona is beautiful desert with vegetation and wildlife, including bighorn sheep and desert tortoise. More than a quarter of Arizona is forests.

In the mid-1800s, fortunes were made when a rich silver lode was discovered in what would become Virginia City, Nevada. Today the former mining town celebrates its past and its desert location with camel races and other events.

LANDSCAPE

The Southwest is famous for its desert landscape, but it also boasts mountain ranges, forest, grassland, plains, and prairie. Texas, the second biggest state in the U.S., has forests, rolling prairies, and dry, high plains. Nevada is a desert state, but among its almost 100 mountain ranges are the Sierra Nevadas, a source of countless rivers.

ECONOMY

The Southwest's clear skies and sunny days attract people and industries, making it one of the nation's fastest-growing regions. High-tech companies that produce microchips, personal computers, and other electronic equipment have settled in the region. Numerous military bases and other federal installations also generate jobs and income. Oil in Texas, silver and gold in Nevada, and natural gas in New Mexico are just some of the natural resources produced by this regional mining powerhouse. Gambling was legalized in Nevada in 1931; the sights, sounds, and opportunities of Las Vegas draw both visitors and permanent residents, making it the fastest-growing city in the nation. The topography and arid climate are ideal for cattle farming, which has long been a staple of the region's economy. The Southwest's cowboy culture is also a big draw for tourists—Old West attractions include legendary Tombstone, Arizona. Crop farming is often a challenge, and yet New Mexico harvests chili peppers and Texas produces cotton, apples, and corn.

1881 Wyatt Earp and his brothers engage in a gun battle with outlaws at the O.K. Corral in Tombstone, Arizona.

1931 Gambling is legalized in Nevada.

1945 The world's first atomic bomb is tested near Alamogordo, New Mexico.

1964 Houston's Manned Spacecraft Center becomes NASA's center for training U.S. astronauts.

STATE FACTS

STATE BIRD
Mountain Bluebird

STATE FLOWER
Sagebrush

STATE TREE
Bristlecone Pine

CAPITAL
Carson City

POPULATION
1,998,257 (2000)

STATEHOOD
October 31, 1864
Rank: 36th

LARGEST CITIES
Las Vegas (478,434)
Reno (180,480)
Henderson (175,381)

LAND AREA
109,826 sq. mi.
(284,449 sq. km.)

NEVADA
the silver state

Some of North America's earliest native cultures lived in Nevada. Rock etchings prove the presence of cave dwellers thousands of years ago. When fur traders and explorers ventured into the area in the early 1800s, they found Mohave, Shoshone, and other American Indians.

In 1830, William Wolfskill cleared a path that came to be known as the Old Spanish Trail, a route from Santa Fe to Los Angeles via the Nevada region. John C. Frémont explored the Sierra Nevada mountains 13 years later and provided information about the land. After the Mexican-American War, the U.S. gained control of the area. More than a decade later, deposits of silver ore were found at the Comstock Lode, leading to the state's nickname. Miners, eager to strike it rich, found the area hard to reach; Nevada's deserts and snow-capped mountains were difficult to cross. The mountains were on the minds of those who chose the state's name—*Nevada* is Spanish for "snowfall."

Today, mining is still important to Nevada's economy. Millions of tourists come each year to visit Nevada's scenic parks, resorts, and tourist sites, including the Hoover Dam and the casinos of the Las Vegas Strip.

NEVADA

●Reno

★CARSON CITY

Lake Tahoe

CALIFORNIA

ALPINE SPLENDOR
Lake Tahoe, on the California-Nevada border, is the largest alpine lake in North America and a major draw for the resort town of the same name. The lake lies 6,228 feet (1,898 m) above sea level in the Sierras, but its great depth of 1,645 feet (501 m) prevents it from freezing over. John Frémont recorded his description of the lake in 1844. He noted the lake's crystal blue clearness, which has since been clouded by pollution. The government began restoring the lake in the late 1990s.

EXTRATERRESTRIAL HIGHWAY
Route 375, a short stretch of highway that lies 100 miles (161 m) to the north of Las Vegas, passes the small town of Rachel. Many UFO believers claim that Rachel is one of the most alien-visited sites in the country. The Extraterrestrial Highway sign attracts tourist attention and brings many people into Rachel and the surrounding historic pioneer territory.

Extraterrestrial Highway
NEVADA 375
©1996 STATE OF NEVADA. All Rights Reserved.

POWER PLAYER
At 726 feet (221 m) tall and 1,244 feet (379 m) long, the Hoover Dam on the Colorado River is one of the world's largest. It provides hydroelectric power to Arizona, California, and Nevada, as well as flood control for local areas. It also brings in water from Lake Mead, the country's largest reservoir, to irrigate parts of Southern California, Arizona, and Mexico.

IDAHO

UTAH

ARIZONA

Ely

Las Vegas

Henderson ● ■ *Hoover Dam*

VIVA LAS VEGAS

By day, the Las Vegas Strip thrives with family-themed amusement rides and air-conditioned casinos. At night, flashing neon lights—and people in equally flashy costumes—welcome adults into nightclubs featuring acts such as Cirque du Soleil.

FIRST LADY FROM NEVADA

PAT NIXON

Born Thelma Catherine Ryan in Ely, Nevada, Pat Nixon was given the nickname by her father who called her his "St. Patrick's babe in the morning." Pat Nixon married future president Richard Nixon, then a lawyer, in 1940. Within a year, the couple moved to Washington, D.C., and then California, following his career path, which included four years in Congress representing the state of California. After her husband won the presidency, Pat Nixon began a literacy program and was the first First Lady to visit a combat zone (South Vietnam in 1969). She died at her home in Park Ridge, New Jersey, in 1993.

Nixon worked as a government economist during World War II.

BRIGHT LIGHTS, BIG MONEY

Nevada legalized gambling in 1931; today gaming is an important part of the state's economy. Las Vegas's casino hotels and entertainment events have earned it the nickname "The Entertainment Capital of the World" and attract millions of people each year. Lake Tahoe and Reno also have popular casinos, and in winter the state's ski resorts attract even more tourists. With so many millions of tourists, it's no surprise half of Nevada's workers are employed in the service industry.

DID YOU KNOW?

On average, 150 couples get married in Las Vegas each day. Couples can choose from dozens of wedding chapels—and can even be married by an Elvis impersonator.

SILVER DOLLARS

Comstock Lode, the richest U.S. silver deposit, was discovered in 1857. Henry T.P. Comstock, who had claimed the land, sold it, thinking it held little profit. Its new owners, however, found vast amounts of silver ore. By 1878 the silver deposits were nearly exhausted. Mining, however, is still big business in Nevada— the state leads the nation in gold, silver, and mercury production.

BULLY FOR BURROS

Donkeys, called *burros* in Spanish, were brought to North America by Spanish explorers, who used them as pack animals. Later, prospectors used them to haul their finds, including silver, gold, and borax. Today, Nevada has the largest wild burro—and wild horse— population in the U.S.

STATE BIRD
Cactus Wren

STATE FLOWER
Saguaro Blossom

STATE TREE
Paloverde

CAPITAL
Phoenix

POPULATION
5,130,632 (2000)

STATEHOOD
February 14, 1912
Rank: 48th

LARGEST CITIES
Phoenix (1,321,045)
Tucson (486,699)
Mesa (396,375)

LAND AREA
113,635 sq. mi.
(294,316 sq. km.)

ARIZONA
the grand canyon state

During the 1530s, Spanish explorers in South America heard legends about the treasure-filled Seven Cities of Cibola. Expeditions were attempted, including several to the Arizona region, seeking the riches. The Spanish never did find them, but they did encounter the Hopi and the Zuni, among other American Indian cultures. The Spanish then established numerous Roman Catholic missions throughout the region, but it wasn't until 1752 that Spanish troops founded Arizona's first permanent settlement at Tubac.

In 1848, the United States took control after the Mexican-American War. The Arizona Territory was created, deriving its name from the American Indian word *Arizonac*, meaning "little spring." Throughout the 1800s, settlers fought with the Apache, who were led by Cochise, Geronimo, and others. During the late 1800s, gold and silver were discovered, as were irrigation tactics that made farming possible in the often dry, hot climate.

Today, tourists visit Arizona to see the majestic Grand Canyon and Monument Valley's sculpted landscape, as well as the animals and plants that thrive in these harsh environments. Historical sites such as Tombstone and newer events, such as the Fiesta Bowl, are also big attractions. Meanwhile, the state's large high-tech industry helps generate income.

WILDLIFE COPES WITH HEAT
The poisonous Gila monster is one of 40 lizard species that find Arizona's hot, dry climate livable. Rare, poisonous coral snakes as well as scorpions are also desert dwellers. Arizona's temperature ranges widely from the mild south to the chillier northern and central mountain areas. In July, temperatures range between 74°F (23°C) and the high 90s (32°C to 37°C), while January averages hover in the 30s to the high 40s (-1°C to 9°C).

A GRAND SIGHT
One of the world's most famous natural settings, the Grand Canyon, is a 277-mile (446-km-) red rock valley. Its walls reveal 21 varied layers of rock formed by the sedimentation of ancient sea life and mud gradually compressing into rock. The oldest visible layer was formed 1.7 billion years ago, while the youngest is 235 million years old.

NATURAL MONUMENT
One of the unique sights found in Monument Valley State Park is the Teardrop Arch rock formation. The park itself lies in a Navajo reservation on the border of northeastern Arizona and southeastern Utah. A featured setting in numerous Western movies, Monument Valley provides some of the southwest's most recognizable landscape in the form of a red-earth desert and jagged rock formations.

UTAH

Monument Valley State Park

GRAND CANYON

Little Colorado River

NEW MEXICO

RIZONA

★ PHOENIX

Tempe • • Mesa

Saguaro National Park

• Tucson

• Tombstone

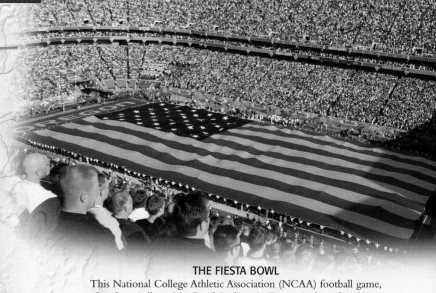

THE FIESTA BOWL

This National College Athletic Association (NCAA) football game, played annually at Sun Devil Stadium in Tempe, is the culmination of several days of celebrations, including a nationally televised parade. The Fiesta Bowl began in 1972 as a charity game for the fight against drug abuse.

LABOR RIGHTS LEADER

CÉSAR ESTRADA CHAVEZ

Born near Yuma, Arizona, César Chavez began working as a migrant farm worker at age 10. He left school in eighth grade to help support his family. After moving to California, he joined the Community Service Organization (CSO) and began coordinating voter registration drives and battling residential racial discrimination. Chavez eventually left the organization to found the National Farm Workers Association to help migrant farm workers gain their rights. In 1994, a year after his death, Chavez received the Presidential Medal of Freedom.

Chavez asked Americans to boycott grapes to help force growers to pay workers higher wages.

AREA OF INDUSTRY

Since World War II, the state's high-tech sector has boomed. Honeywell's aerospace business, headquartered in Phoenix, boasts total sales of $9.7 billion. Other high-tech companies include Boeing, Intel, and Motorola.

DID YOU KNOW?

London Bridge, which once spanned London's Thames River, today stands in Lake Havasu City, Arizona.

DESERT PLANTS

Many cacti varieties thrive in southern Arizona's vast desert areas, particularly the Saguaro cacti in Saguaro National Park, which lies near Tucson. Saguro cacti can grow as tall as 50 feet (15 m)—bigger than any other cactus species in the nation. Its blossom is the state flower. Cacti are well suited for southwestern Arizona's average of 2 to 5 inches (5 to 13 cm) of rain a year. Not all of Arizona is desert, however. Forests featuring ponderosa pines and Douglas firs cover more than a fourth of the state, and wildflowers grow in the high mountains.

THE REAL DEAL WILD WEST

Tombstone is a major tourist attraction due to its reputation as a rough border town during the days of the "Wild" West. The town includes a cemetery known as Boot Hill because the cowboys buried there "died with their boots on."

STATE BIRD
Roadrunner

STATE FLOWER
Yucca

STATE TREE
Piñon

CAPITAL
Santa Fe

POPULATION
1,819,046 (2000)

STATEHOOD
January 6, 1912
Rank: 47th

LARGEST CITIES
Albuquerque (448,607)
Las Cruces (74,267)
Santa Fe (62,203)

LAND AREA
121,356 sq. mi.
(314,312 sq. km.)

NEW MEXICO
the land of enchantment

Between 1528 and 1536, Álvar Núñez Cabeza de Vaca of Spain was the first European to explore what is now New Mexico. He came into contact with both the Navajo and Apache people who lived on the land. Francisco Vásquez de Coronado claimed the land for Spain in 1537. After Mexico separated from Spain in 1821, it took control of the region and gave it its name. As a result of its victory in the Mexican-American War, the U.S. gained control of New Mexico.

Modern New Mexico is popular among tourists for its scenic beauty and historical landmarks. Among its most popular historical sites is Bandelier National Monument, which features hundreds of cliff dwellings built by the Anasazi, ancient peoples who lived in the region. New Mexico is also the site of the first atomic bomb test. Some tourists are lured by the state's possible alien connection, as decades of rumors mark Roswell and other desert sites as active alien landing areas.

Mountain ranges, canyons, and rocky deserts cover much of the state, which is why it is lightly populated. Spanish traditions and food remain part of the state's culture, partly because more than one-third of the population is Hispanic—a higher percentage than any other state. American Indian culture is also important, as many tribes still live in pueblos around the region.

Today, New Mexico is a leading mining state—natural gas and various ores are among its key mineral products. Low rainfall and rough land prevent widespread crop farming, but the state is the country's top producer of chili peppers. Companies such as Intel and Honeywell make New Mexico their home, making technology an important part of the state's economy.

BANDELIER NATIONAL MONUMENT
Hundreds of Anasazi cliff dwellings and pueblo-style homes are scattered across the Pajarito Plateau of northern New Mexico. The Anasazi, ancient American Indians, lived in the region from the eleventh to the fourteenth century A.D. They are ancestors of the present Pueblo people, and their cliff dwellings are the focus of Bandelier National Monument. Visitors can explore these ancient dwellings and also hike, bird-watch, and camp along the ground's 70 miles (113 km) of trails.

SAN MIGUEL MISSION SOCORRO
The Spanish established missions, or churches, to help stake their claims to territory in both North and South America. The missions were intended to convert American Indians to Christianity. San Miguel Mission Socorro, established in 1692, is an authentic mix of Spanish-style architecture and American Indian-created design. Piro Indians hand-carved and painted the ceiling beams inside the mission.

COLORADO

Rio Grande

Bandelier National Monument

jarito lateau

■ •Los Alamos

★ SANTA FE

•Rio Rancho

Rio Grande

San Miguel Mission

NEW MEXICO

•Roswell

SAN ANDRES MOUNTAINS

•Alamogordo

•Artesia

•Carlsbad

Las Cruces

Rio Grande

TEXAS

TEXAS

•Clovis

•Hobbs

ATOMIC BOMB TEST

The Los Alamos National Laboratory was established in 1943, mainly to serve as the secret site where the U.S. government developed the first atomic bomb. The first atomic bomb, or A-bomb, test was conducted at Trinity Site near the city of Alamogordo on July 16, 1945. The following month, two bombs made at Los Alamos were dropped on Japan, killing 140,000 people and leading Japan to surrender, ending World War II.

IT'S ALL IN THE CHIP

Arizona's economy is partially fueled by high technology—computer and electronics companies provide 80 percent of the state's manufacturing revenue. Among Arizona's high-tech companies is Intel, which produces microchips.

POTTERY PARADE

Women from Zuni Pueblo, located in western New Mexico, take part in the annual Gallup Indian Ceremonial. They carry the distinctive pottery they craft on their heads. Each of New Mexico's pueblos and tribes has developed its own pottery style, in many cases based on the techniques and designs of their ancestors.

DID YOU KNOW?

The first road created in the U.S. by Europeans was El Camino Real, which stretched from Santa Fe to Mexico City, Mexico. Parts of it still exist.

ROSWELL CITY LIMITS

The city of Roswell has become an international attraction—tourists flock to the place where, supposedly, an alien spaceship crashed on July 4, 1947. A once-secret Air Force test site known as Area 51, located nearby, has added to the region's mystique.

PAINTER OF THE DESERT

GEORGIA O'KEEFFE

Artist Georgia O'Keeffe first visited New Mexico in 1929. She loved the scenic horizons and stark landscape and began visiting the state each summer thereafter to paint. In 1949 she moved to Taos and lived there until her death at age 98. O'Keeffe's pioneering vision is best preserved in her large-scale, lush oil paintings of flowers and of the desert.

O'Keeffe's eyesight began to fail when she was in her 70s. Thereafter she sculpted, sketched, and painted watercolors.

DESERT, BUT NOT DESERTED

Much of New Mexico is rugged land that receives little rainfall. Low rainfall and rough land do not allow for much crop farming. The climate is generally warm and dry—July temperatures statewide average 74°F (23°C) though desert temperatures average 105°F (41°C). In January, temperatures drop to an average of 34°F (1°C) and nights are particularly chilly in the high mountains where up to 300 inches (762 cm) of snow can fall each year.

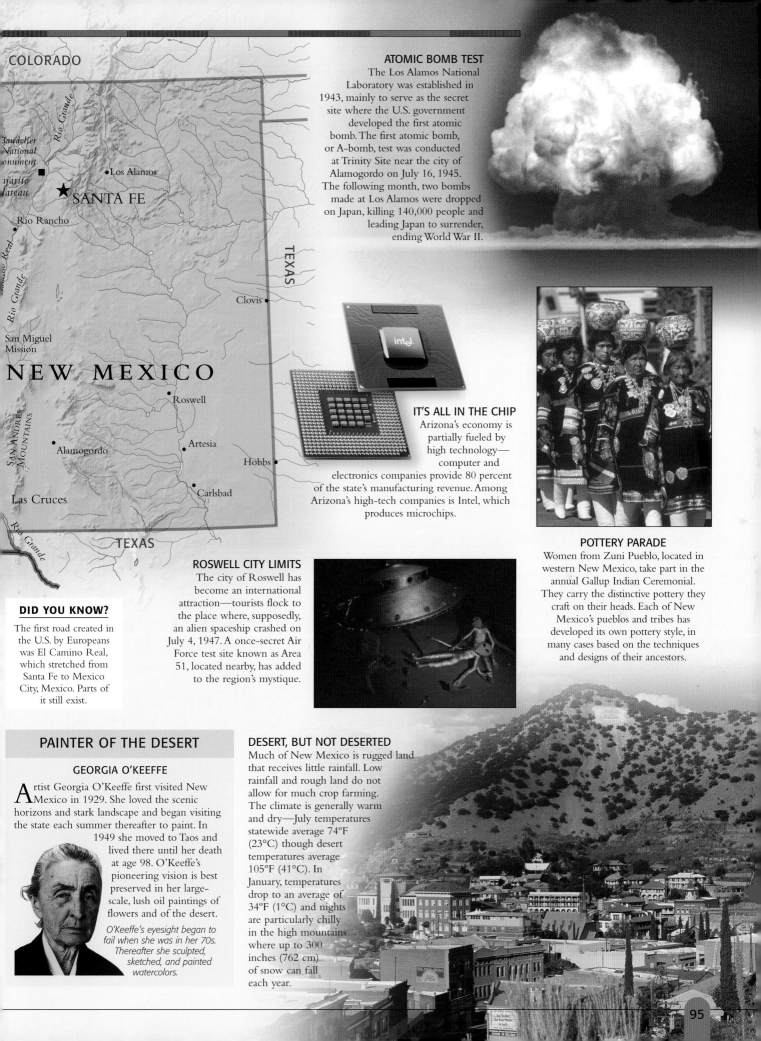

95

STATE BIRD
Mockingbird

STATE FLOWER
Bluebonnet

STATE TREE
Pecan

CAPITAL
Austin

POPULATION
20,851,820 (2000)

STATEHOOD
December 29, 1845
Rank: 28th

LARGEST CITIES
Houston (1,953,631)
Dallas (1,188,580)
San Antonio (1,144,646)

LAND AREA
261,797 sq. mi.
(678,054 sq. km.)

TEXAS
the lone star state

HIGH-TECH SPACE BOOM
Texas's high-tech boom began in 1961 when NASA opened its space center in Houston. Above, astronauts train underwater for a shuttle mission. The underwater environment is the closest thing on Earth to the weightless environment of space.

Spanish explorers such as Francisco Vásquez Coronado traveled through Texas between 1528 and 1542, encountering Comanche, Apache, and other American Indians. The first European settlement, however, wasn't established until 1682, when settlers from Spain established the mission Ysleta at present-day El Paso. The Spanish founded several more Roman Catholic missions, or churches, soon thereafter.

In 1685, French explorer René-Robert Cavelier, Sieur de La Salle arrived in east Texas. In 1690, the Spanish founded a mission there—Francisco de los Tejas—to counter France's claim to the land. The Spanish used the American Indian word *tejas*, meaning "friends" or "allies," to refer to the area, leading to the state's name.

By the early 1800s, Mexico controlled Texas. The Mexican government invited U.S. settlers into the area, and Stephen F. Austin established the first U.S. settlement. By 1830, Americans flocking to the region outnumbered Mexican settlers by three to one. The Americans eventually petitioned Mexico to become a separate Mexican state. The Texas Revolution, which began in 1835, was sparked in part by Mexico's refusal to allow the American settlers to own slaves. The war peaked with the defense of San Antonio's Alamo, and ended with the battle of San Jacinto on April 21, 1836. After 10 years of independence, Texas became part of the U.S. By 1901, oil was discovered and the economy boomed. Oil as well as agriculture and high technology continue to fuel the Texas economy.

LONG-TIME LAW ENFORCERS
The Texas Rangers began as a fighting force that upheld the law in Texas. Originally, they consisted of three companies of 25 men each, but their numbers grew. They served as scouts and fighters during the Mexican-American War and later attempted to control problems with outlaws. In 1935, the Rangers were merged with the state highway patrol.

REMEMBER THE ALAMO!
On February 24, 1835, a battle broke out between 180 American settlers who held the Alamo, a former mission, and the Mexican Army. The battle ended with the deaths of the fort's defenders on March 6, including frontiersman Davey Crockett. The Americans later defeated the Mexicans at San Jacinto amid cries of "Remember the Alamo!" Today, the Alamo is a major tourist site for San Antonio.

CATTLE COUNTRY

Longhorn cattle have been the basis of the state's economy for more than 100 years. Now joined by other varieties, beef cattle provide more than 60 percent of the state's annual agricultural income. The state's mild climate, rich grasslands, and water resources make it a natural for raising cattle, as well as sheep and lambs.

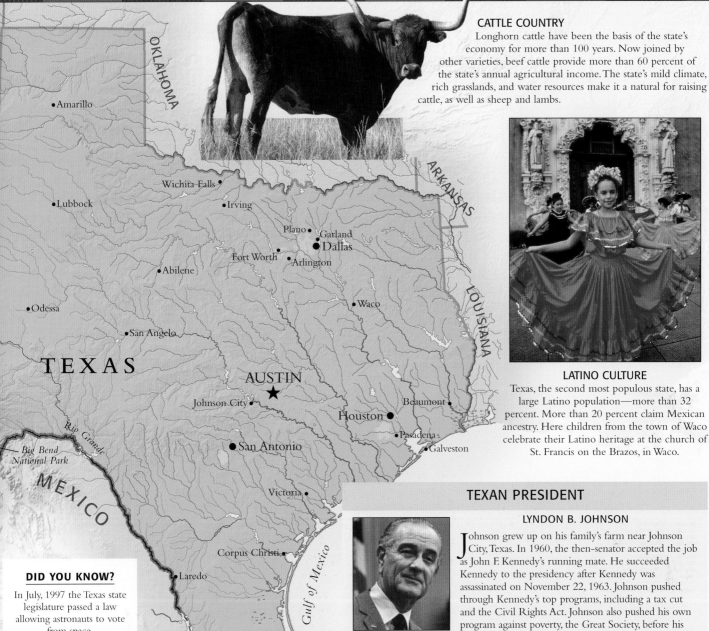

OKLAHOMA

• Amarillo

• Lubbock

Wichita Falls •

• Irving

Plano • • Garland
Fort Worth • **Dallas**
• Abilene • Arlington

ARKANSAS

• Odessa

• San Angelo

• Waco

LOUISIANA

TEXAS

★ AUSTIN

Johnson City •

Beaumont •

Houston •

Rio Grande
Big Bend
National Park

San Antonio

• Pasadena
• Galveston

MEXICO

Victoria •

Gulf of Mexico

Corpus Christi •

• Laredo

LATINO CULTURE

Texas, the second most populous state, has a large Latino population—more than 32 percent. More than 20 percent claim Mexican ancestry. Here children from the town of Waco celebrate their Latino heritage at the church of St. Francis on the Brazos, in Waco.

TEXAN PRESIDENT

LYNDON B. JOHNSON

Johnson grew up on his family's farm near Johnson City, Texas. In 1960, the then-senator accepted the job as John F. Kennedy's running mate. He succeeded Kennedy to the presidency after Kennedy was assassinated on November 22, 1963. Johnson pushed through Kennedy's top programs, including a tax cut and the Civil Rights Act. Johnson also pushed his own program against poverty, the Great Society, before his reelection in November 1964. In August of 1964, the president escalated the military campaign against South Vietnam to stop communists from gaining power.

Johnson retired from political life due to the unpopular Vietnam War.

BIG BEND BORDER

Along the U.S.-Mexico border lies Big Bend National Park. The Chisos Mountains, the Rio Grande, the Chihuahan Desert, petrified trees, and deep canyons such as the Santa Elena provide the park with diverse scenery. While the lower Rio Grande valley is generally warmer than the rest of the state, Texas's average temperatures range from about 46°F (8°C) in January to 83°F (28°C) in July.

DID YOU KNOW?

In July, 1997 the Texas state legislature passed a law allowing astronauts to vote from space.

BORDER CROSSINGS AND TRADE

The 43 border crossings between Texas and Mexico are among the busiest in the U.S. Most of the crossings are economy-oriented, including the import and export of goods and food products. In 2000, U.S. exports to Mexico topped $110 billion, while imports from Mexico were more than $135 billion. Today Texas is the state that exports the most goods to Mexico.

THE ROCKY MOUNTAIN STATES

The Anasazi culture was established in Colorado and Utah about two thousand years ago; these people left behind remarkable cliff dwellings and other structures throughout the region. The Lewis and Clark Expedition mapped much of the Rocky Mountain region between 1804 and 1806. The rugged, mountainous landscape posed considerable challenges to the fur traders, miners, and farmers who came long after them.

Silver City, Idaho, was a thriving mining town in the late 1800s and is now one of the region's most popular "ghost" towns.

There were few white settlers in the region until the 1850s, when gold, silver, and other precious minerals were discovered. The Rocky Mountain region is overwhelmingly rural, based on the region's topography and the major economic activities of farming, ranching, and mining conducted throughout these states. Denver and Salt Lake City are two of the Rocky Mountains' major urban centers. In addition to the jagged peaks and massive plateaus of the Rockies, the Rocky Mountain states include the great plains of eastern Montana, Wyoming, and Colorado, as well as the Great Salt Lake desert in Utah.

LANDSCAPE

Stretching from southern Canada to central New Mexico, the Rocky Mountains are North America's largest mountain range and the source for the Colorado, Snake, and other major rivers. Mt. Elbert in Colorado is the highest peak at 14,433 feet (4,399 m). While the Rockies define western Colorado, Wyoming, and Montana, in the east are arid, grass-covered plains suitable for farming and ranching—wheat, corn, cattle and sheep are raised there. Southern Idaho's fertile farmland produces potatoes, peas, and other crops. The landscape of the Rocky Mountain states also contains evidence of prehistoric cultures, including 800-year-old carvings and images on Newspaper Rock in Utah.

William "Buffalo Bill" Cody was an accomplished hunter, soldier, and horseman who first created his Wild West show in 1883. This show, filled with cowboys and Indians, strongly influenced perceptions of life on the western frontier.

KEY DATES

1000 The Anasazi begin building cliff houses throughout the region. Many of these dwellings still exist today.

1804 The Lewis and Clark Expedition begins to map the region.

1847 Brigham Young leads the Mormons to Utah. They establish Salt Lake City.

CLIMATE

A wide range of climates prevail in this region, from Montana's mild summer average of 64°F to 71°F (18°C to 22°C) to a blistering 100°F (38°C) and higher in the Great Salt Lake Desert of Utah. The Rockies have a major impact on climate, with conditions growing colder and more extreme at higher elevations. Many of the Rockies's highest peaks remain snow-covered for much of the year. Winter conditions are extremely variable on the eastern slope of the Rockies due to the warm, dry Chinook winds, which can raise the temperature considerably in a matter of hours.

About 8,500 Pikuni of the Blackfleet Nation live on the Blackfeet Indian Reservation in northern Montana, which hosts the annual North American Indian Days celebration.

Much of the rugged terrain of the region is unsuitable for crop farming, but cattle ranching has thrived in the Rocky Mountains and on the plains since the 1860s.

LIFESTYLE

William "Buffalo Bill" Cody's Wild West shows celebrated the American West. Today, Western heritage is preserved in deserted mining towns that welcome tourists, such as Silver City, Idaho, and in the region's many rodeos. Winter sports are a considerable draw for residents and visitors alike. The quality of snow and slopes draws skiers to resorts such as Sun Valley, Idaho, and Aspen and Vail, Colorado. The glacier-covered peaks and abundant wildlife of Wyoming's Grand Tetons are an example of the region's natural beauty. American Indian culture is celebrated in events such as the yearly Crow Fair held in Montana.

Mormons, meanwhile, have played a central role in Utah's development and culture since Brigham Young established the state's first Mormon settlement in 1847.

ECONOMY

Mining, lumber, cattle, crop farming, and tourism are important industries in the Rocky Mountain states. Silver, lead, coal, and platinum are among the many minerals extracted in this region. The forests of the Rockies yield much income for the timber industry. Beef cattle and sheep account for much of the agricultural output; corn, potatoes, wheat, and other grains are some of the major crops. Tourist dollars are another important source of income. From the high, treeless plains of western Montana to the dramatic canyon vistas of Idaho's Highway 95, the landscape of these states is sure to thrill every viewer.

Professional and amateur skiers from around the world come to the Rocky Mountain states to experience the region's world-class slopes.

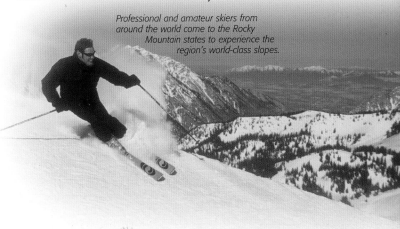

1869 The first transcontinental railroad, extending from the East Coast to the West Coast, is completed. The two lines join up at Promontory Point, Utah.

1876 Dakota (Sioux) and Cheyenne forces in Montana defeat U.S. military forces in the Battle of the Little Big Horn.

1913 Carl Howelson builds the first ski jump at Steamboat Springs, Colorado.

1955 Arco, Idaho, becomes the first U.S. town to be lit completely by atomic power.

STATE BIRD
Mountain Bluebird

STATE FLOWER
Syringa

STATE TREE
Western White Pine

CAPITAL
Boise

POPULATION
1,293,953 (2000)

STATEHOOD
July 3, 1890
Rank: 43rd

LARGEST CITIES
Boise (185,787)
Nampa (51,867)
Pocatello (51,466)

LAND AREA
82,747 sq. mi.
(214,315 sq. km.)

IDAHO

the gem state

Idaho's first inhabitants included the Shoshone, Coeur d'Alene, and Bannock cultures. It is unknown how Idaho got its name, but it may be derived from the Shoshone exclamation *e-dah-how,* meaning "it is sun up" or "gem of the mountains."

In 1805 Meriwether Lewis and William Clark became the first white people to explore the region. Four years later, Canadian David Thompson built a fur-trading post on the shores of Lake Pend Oreille. It wasn't until 1860, however, that Franklin, the first permanent settlement, was founded. That same year, prospector E. D. Pierce found gold in Orofino Creek.

The land's fertile soil, rich mineral deposits, Rocky Mountain peaks, and many lakes and rivers are products of age-old volcanic activity and glacial movement. Though miners and farmers journeyed to the area to take advantage of this mineral-rich land, only farmers stayed. Today, Idaho produces both potatoes and trout for the nation's table. The state's rural roots are never forgotten, as seen in regional festivals such as Ketchum's Trailing of the Sheep, while tourists arrive from around the globe for both outdoor adventures and to visit unique natural settings, such as Craters of the Moon.

HOT SPOT
Craters of the Moon National Monument resembles the landscape of the Moon so much that NASA once used the area for astronaut training. Formed by volcanoes 15,000 years ago, the landscape is far from barren. Sagebrush and twisted trees dot its dark landscape.

CANADA

WASHINGTON

Coeur d'Alene

Moscow

Lewiston

MONTANA

BITTERROOT RANGE

Whitewater Grade

OREGON

HELLS CANYON

Snake River

IDAHO

BOISE

Sun Valley

Ketchum

Nampa

Snake River

Triumph

OWYHEE MTS

NEVADA

POTATOES PLUS
About one-fourth of Idaho is farmland, consisting of close to 24,500 farms. Idaho grows one-third of the nation's potatoes, more than any other state. The potatoes are harvested in early fall and trucks help haul them to every state in the nation. In 1998, that was 13.8 billion pounds (6.26 billion kg). Eighty percent of McDonald's French fries are cut from potatoes grown near Boise. Other Idaho crops include winter peas, hay, wheat, and beef.

FISH FOR FINANCE
The majority of the nation's commercially raised trout is raised in Idaho, where this game fish also thrives in the state's many rivers, lakes, and streams. Rainbow trout are most common, but speckled, brown, cutthroat (the state fish), golden, and Dolly Varden are also caught. Other local fish filling the waters include salmon in Salmon River and perch, bass, and catfish.

SPEEDY STREET

PICABO STREET

In 2001, *Sports Illustrated* named Picabo Street one of the top 50 female athletes of all time. Born in the tiny Rocky Mountain town of Triumph on April 3, 1971, Street began skiing at age six, and made the U.S. Ski Team eleven years later. In 1993, she won a silver medal in the world championships, following it up with silver at the 1994 Olympics. In 1995, she became the first American ever to win a World Cup title. She won the title again in 1996, and another world championship title as well.

After injuring her knee in December 1996, Street recovered, and later won gold in the super giant slalom at the 1998 Olympics. Further knee injuries forced Street into retirement after the 2002 Olympics.

Picabo means "shining waters" in the Sho-Ban language.

SKI PARADISE

With an average of 60 inches (152 cm) of snow each year, Idaho is a haven for skiers. Sun Valley, the state's best known ski resort, is the site of the world's first ski lift. Other big ski resorts include Pebble Creek, near Pocatello, and Bogus Basin, near Boise. Along with white water sports and camping, skiing brings tourist money to the economy and has created many service-related jobs. Temperatures in the state range from an average of a frosty 23°F (-5°C) in January to 67°F (19°C) in July.

DID YOU KNOW?

The longest main street in the U.S. is a 33-mile (53 km-) long road in Island Park, Idaho.

SHEEP ON THE RUN

Mid-October in the mountain town of Ketchum, Idaho, brings a parade of 1,700 sheep down Main Street, past boutiques, hotels, restaurants, and a cheering crowd. The sheep are part of the annual three-day Trailing of the Sheep Festival, which celebrates the century-old tradition of shepherds moving their flocks from summer pastures around Ketchum and Sun Valley south to winter grazing areas.

Island Park
WYOMING
e River Plain
Snake River
lackfoot
Pocatello
UTAH

RIVER RESOURCES

The canyons lining the 1,038-mile (1,670-km) Snake River include the world's deepest—Hells Canyon. The river is also a source of recreational enjoyment and an important natural resource; its water is used to irrigate the surrounding farmland. The river forms part of Idaho's border with Oregon.

FORMED BY FIRE...AND ICE

Along the much-traveled roads of Whitebird Grade and Highway 95, Idaho's steep canyons sink to 8,023 feet (2,445 m), while snow-capped peaks rise to heights of 12,000 feet (3,658 m). The landscape includes ancient lava flows, vast desert areas, and bodies of water that were formed by earthquakes, volcanic eruptions, and glaciers. Millions of years later, melting glaciers flooded the area and carved steep canyons and gorges in the northern part of the state. Idaho's rugged landscape also includes the Rocky Mountains and the desertlike Great Basin of the southeast.

STATE BIRD
Western Meadowlark

STATE FLOWER
Bitterroot

STATE TREE
Ponderosa Pine

CAPITAL
Helena

POPULATION
902,195 (2000)

STATEHOOD
November 8, 1889
Rank: 41st

LARGEST CITIES
Billings (89,847)
Missoula (57,053)
Great Falls (56,690)

LAND AREA
145,552 sq. mi.
(376,980 sq. km.)

MONTANA

MONTANA
big sky country

WILD WATER
For every age and ability, Montana has some of the best white water on its many rivers. One way to see Glacier National Park is to kayak through it.

The Montana region was populated by Blackfoot, Sioux, Shoshone, and Cheyenne, among others, when most of the state was granted to the U.S. under the Louisiana Purchase of 1803. Two years later, Lewis and Clark and their exploration party were perhaps the first whites to enter the area. The first permanent white settlement—a trading post—was established four years later, when Canadian and American fur traders began to enter the territory.

Settlers began to trickle in during a gold rush in 1852, but permanent settlements were rare due to the area's vast wilderness and mountainous setting. In fact, Montana's name comes from the Spanish word *montaña*, which means mountain.

In 1866, the first cattle were brought to the region's extensive grasslands; more populous settlements followed. Today, mining, cattle ranching, and wilderness areas are vital parts of Montana's culture and economy. From Custer's Last Stand to numerous modern Indian reservations, and varied mountainous and plains landscape, Montana's historic people and land are part of its modern appeal.

DID YOU KNOW?
Montana's combined elk, deer, and antelope populations outnumber humans.

WANDERING WILDLIFE
Big game animals such as elk, mule deer, black bear, and cougars roam through western Montana, while the remote mountain areas are home to scores of grizzly bears, Rocky Mountain goats, bighorn sheep, and moose. Millions of buffalo once filled the state, but now those that have survived are found only in the National Bison Range in the Flathead Valley and smaller protected areas. Montana has 380 bird species, including one of the last remaining trumpeter swan populations, which live in Red Rocks Lakes National Wildlife Refuge.

DEFEAT AT LITTLE BIG HORN
On June 25, 1876, the Dakota (Sioux) and Northern Cheyenne defeated the U.S. Seventh Calvary. The event is often called Custer's Last Stand because it was General George Armstrong Custer who led more than 200 soldiers to their deaths. Their bodies were buried on the battlefield.

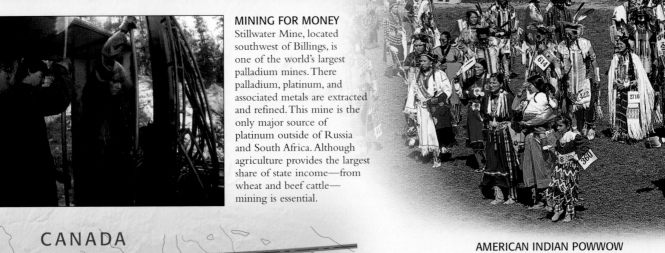

MINING FOR MONEY

Stillwater Mine, located southwest of Billings, is one of the world's largest palladium mines. There palladium, platinum, and associated metals are extracted and refined. This mine is the only major source of platinum outside of Russia and South Africa. Although agriculture provides the largest share of state income—from wheat and beef cattle—mining is essential.

AMERICAN INDIAN POWWOW

Every August the Crow Reservation, southeast of Billings, is the site of the annual Crow Fair. One of North America's largest powwows, the event draws thousands of American Indians. Participants camp along the Little Big Horn River and enjoy a rodeo, a native dance competition, wild horse races, parades, and tribal reunions. About 56,000 American Indians live in Montana, mostly on reservations.

FIRST ELECTED CONGRESSWOMAN

JEANNETTE RANKIN

Pacifist and women's rights advocate Jeannette Rankin became the country's first female congresswoman in 1916. Rankin was born on a Montana ranch in 1880. In her early 20s, she began a quest to make her state one of the first to allow women the right to vote. Her hopes became reality in 1914, four years before women had the right to vote nationwide. Two years later, Rankin successfully campaigned as a Republican for a seat in the U.S. House of Representatives. There, she helped draft a constitutional amendment that would have given all women the right to vote, although the Senate later defeated it. Rankin was elected to Congress again in 1940.

At age 86, Rankin led a march on Washington to protest the Vietnam War.

CANADA

• Havre

• Fort Peck

MONTANA

NORTH DAKOTA

S. DAKOTA

Billings

Crow
Reservation

Little Big Horn
Battlefield

Stillwater Mine

WYOMING

GLACIERS AND PEAKS

Filling Glacier National Park are 2,000 lakes, thick forests, wide meadows, and more than 50 glaciers. While the average July temperature in the state is a mild 64°F to 71°F (18°C to 22°C), the average January temperature dips to between 14°F and 20°F (-10°C and -7°C). The eastern section of the state and high mountain areas are always colder. Temperatures are widely affected by Chinook winds. This weather phenomenon is caused when wind and air pressure increases as it moves from higher to lower elevations. Chinook winds can cause huge temperature increases in just a few hours.

ROCKY VISTA

The glacier-formed sandstone rock structures of Jerusalem Rocks, on Montana's Canadian border, are representative of half of Montana's scenery. The western half is similarly mountainous, while the eastern half is part of the broad Great Plains, drained by the Missouri River, which begins in southwest Montana. The Bitterroot Range, part of the Rocky Mountains, marks Montana's western boundary.

STATE BIRD
Western Meadowlark

STATE FLOWER
Indian Paintbrush

STATE TREE
Cottonwood

CAPITAL
Cheyenne

POPULATION
493,782 (2000)

STATEHOOD
July 10, 1890
Rank: 44th

LARGEST CITIES
Cheyenne (53,011)
Casper (49,644)
Laramie (27,204)

LAND AREA
97,100 sq. mi.
(251,489 sq. km.)

WYOMING
the equality state

Wyoming's first inhabitants were paleo-Indians that probably arrived in the area around 9000 B.C. More than 10,000 years later, Native American cultures, including the Crow and Shoshone, made Wyoming their home. Cheyenne, Flathead, and Nez Perce migrated to the area in the 1700s and 1800s, attracted to the bison and other large game animals that lived on the land.

The first written accounts of Wyoming were published in 1811 by John Coulter, an American trapper whose tales encouraged other trappers to migrate there. Others who traveled to the area in the mid-1800s included John C. Frémont, the Mormons on their way to Utah, and prospectors in search of gold in California. Many were interested in the region's mountains and natural resources, but it was later settlers who established cattle ranches on Wyoming's plains.

The name Wyoming means "on the plains" in the language of the Leni-Lenape, American Indians who once lived along the Atlantic Coast. The state's nickname came later, when the state became the first to pass a law giving women the right to vote.

Today, the state's culture is based on its rural setting. Rodeo is the sport of choice. Beef cattle live on many farms, while varied wildlife roam the plains. The state's mountainous settings were created by glaciers and ancient volcanic activity.

ANCIENT VOLCANO
Formed millions of years ago when an extinct volcano eroded, Devils Tower is a core of twisted lava that rises 867 feet (264 m) out of the rocky landscape south of Hulett, Wyoming. The tower was a landmark for settlers traveling west on the Oregon Trail. In 1906, President Theodore Roosevelt made it the country's first national monument.

MANIFEST DESTINY
Settlers making their way west had to pass through Wyoming's mountains and treeless plains via the Oregon trail, which ran along the North Platte River. Their heavy wagons were packed with food, clothing, and children while adults and teens ran alongside them herding horses, cows, pigs, and sheep. Traces of the Oregon Trail include names carved in the cliff by pioneers as well as deep ruts on the prairie left by their wagons.

EQUALITY FOR WOMEN
Two months after the Wyoming Territory's first legislature met in October 1869, a law was passed to offer women over age 21 the right to vote and hold elected office. Legislators passed the law to encourage more women to settle in the state in order to increase the territory's meager population of 8,000. Wyoming was the first state to grant women these rights.

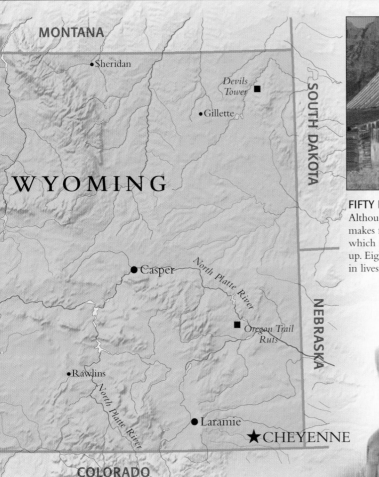

MONTANA

Sheridan

Devils Tower ■

Gillette

WYOMING

Casper

North Platte River

Oregon Trail Ruts ■

Rawlins

North Platte River

Laramie

★ CHEYENNE

SOUTH DAKOTA

NEBRASKA

COLORADO

FIFTY PERCENT FARMLAND

Although half of Wyoming is ranch and farmland, the state's lack of rainfall makes farming a challenge. Many farmers practice dry farming, a technique in which fields may lie unplanted for a year to allow moisture in the soil to build up. Eighty percent of the state's farming income lies in livestock production, especially cattle.

WILDLIFE

Wyoming's plains are home to numerous wildlife species, including swift moving pronghorn antelope, which roam in small herds. The rare black-footed ferret also lives throughout the state. Meanwhile Yellowstone National Park is home to wolves, grizzly bears, and a small herd of bison.

WILD WEST SHOWMAN

WILLIAM FREDERIC CODY

After William Frederic Cody's father died in 1857, he left home to earn money for his family by working for a train company. Two years later he began a series of jobs—with the Pony Express, as an army scout, and as a buffalo hunter for the railroads—that became the basis for the tall-tales later told about him. In 1883, Cody organized Buffalo Bill's Wild West Show, a touring show. Cody established the town of Cody, Wyoming, with a land grant from state officials who hoped Cody's image would attract tourism and settlers.

Cody is buried on Mt. Lookout near Golden, Colorado.

MOUNTAINS AND GLACIERS

The Grand Teton's 12 peaks and glaciers make up the youngest range in the Rockies. The glaciers stay solid thanks to the state's cold winter climate, which averages between 12°F and 22°F (-11°C and -6°C) in January. Still, in the high northwestern mountains, there are much colder temperatures and up to 260 inches (660 cm) of snow per year. July averages a warm, dry 59°F to 71°F (15°C to 22°C).

STATE FACTS

STATE BIRD
Seagull

STATE FLOWER
Sego Lily

STATE TREE
Blue Spruce

CAPITAL
Salt Lake City

POPULATION
2,233,169 (2000)

STATEHOOD
January 4, 1896
Rank: 45th

LARGEST CITIES
Salt Lake City (181,743)
West Valley City (108,896)
Provo (105,166)

LAND AREA
82,144 sq. mi.
(212,753 sq. km.)

UTAH

the beehive state

Ancient people, including the Anasazi, first settled the Utah region several thousand years ago. The Navajo settled there in the late 1600s, while two Spanish expeditions in 1765 and 1776 encountered the Ute, among other native peoples. American fur traders entered Utah for the first time in 1811.

The first whites to establish permanent settlements were the Mormons, members of the Church of Jesus Christ of Latter-Day Saints. Brigham Young organized their settlement of the region in 1847. In 1848, after the Mexican-American War, the U.S. took control of the land. The region was named for the Ute. Utah grew more populated when the first transcontinental railroad was completed in 1869.

Mormons are still important to Utah's culture— they make up 70 percent of the population. The Mormon Tabernacle choir has gained recognition around the world for its musical performances. Utah's modern economy is boosted by tourists who enjoy the state's rugged landscape with remarkable sandstone structures as well as the north's lush snowfall. The winter weather attracted the 2002 Olympics to Salt Lake City. Temperatures vary greatly throughout the state. In January, the north averages 20°F (-7°C), while the southwest averages 39°F (16°C). In July, the Salt Lake City area hits the 60°F (16°C) range as the southwest averages 84°F (29°C).

IDAHO

Golden Spike National Historic Site

Great Salt Lake

SALT LAKE CITY ★

Bonneville Salt Flats

West Valley City ●

Great Salt Lake Desert

Provo ●

NEVADA

UTAH

Sevier Lake

SAWATCH RANGE

Rainbow B National Mon

ARIZONA

NATIVE ROCK ART
The flat sandstone of Newspaper Rock, near Monticello, is covered with more than 350 petroglyphs. They include images of people riding horses and shooting arrows. Scientists have determined that some of the carvings were made more than 800 years ago by ancient native cultures.

GOLDEN SPIKE NATIONAL HISTORIC SITE
Golden Spike National Historic Site in Promontory Point features replicas of old-time steam locomotives and an annual re-creation of the transcontinental railroad's completion. The railroad, completed in 1869, linked the country's east and west coasts.

DID YOU KNOW?

Utah's Rainbow Bridge National Monument is the largest natural bridge in the world. It is 290 feet (88 m) tall.

WYOMING

ROCKY MOUNTAINS

COLORADO

Colorado River

Monticello

Canyonlands
National Park

ake Powell

NM

SALT FLATS

The Bonneville Salt Flats and the Great Salt Lake are remnants of Lake Bonneville, a now dried-up body of water that, during the last Ice Age, was as big as lake Michigan. The area's desert conditions provide a wide range of sometimes brutal temperatures, ranging from 100°F (38°C) in summer to below 0°F (–18°C) in winter.

MORMON TABERNACLE CHOIR

The nearly 400-member Mormon Tabernacle Choir has received international acclaim for its weekly radio broadcasts, made since 1929. The choir's broadcasts are made from the Mormon Tabernacle, a concert hall that features an organ with 11,000 pipes.

2002 OLYMPICS

Seventy-eight events made the XIX Olympics in Salt Lake City the largest winter games to date. Nearly 2,400 athletes from around the world competed from February 8–February 24, 2002. Snow-oriented sportspeople have long been drawn to northern Utah for its impressive snowfall and unspoiled terrain. Alta, a ski area near Salt Lake City, is typically hit with more than 400 inches (1,016 cm) of snow each year.

MORMON LEADER

BRIGHAM YOUNG

Born in 1801 in Whitingham, Vermont, Brigham Young was baptized into the Mormon faith in 1832. He then aided founder Joseph Smith by leading a group of Mormons to their early community at Kirkland, Ohio. Young became a group leader when he was named to the Council of Twelve (Apostles). The Mormons were often attacked for their beliefs, which led to their constant resettling in new communities. Young organized a group move to Nauvoo, Illinois, in the 1830s. After Smith was killed in 1844, Young became the Mormons's spiritual leader. In 1846, he led the Mormons west to settle Salt Lake City and other cities and towns in Utah.

Young was the first governor of the Utah Territory.

CANYONLANDS NATIONAL PARK

Canyonlands National Park is Utah's largest park, spreading over 525 square miles (1,340 sq km) at the place where the Green and Colorado Rivers meet. Red rock canyons, cliffs, arches, and wild rivers mark the scenery. The park isn't easy to visit. It has no paved roads and limited water supplies, so it's difficult for sightseers to get there unless they hike, raft, or travel by jeep.

STATE FACTS

STATE BIRD
Lark Bunting

STATE FLOWER
Rocky Mountain Columbine

STATE TREE
Blue Spruce

CAPITAL
Denver

POPULATION
4,301,261 (2000)

STATEHOOD
August 1, 1876
Rank: 38th

LARGEST CITIES
Denver (554,636)
Colorado Springs (360,890)
Aurora (276,393)

LAND AREA
103,718 sq. mi.
(268,630 sq. km.)

COLORADO

the rocky mountain state

Colorado's natural wonders attract people who want to ski, snowboard, and enjoy rugged natural surroundings. The state has numerous forest areas and flat plains, on which sheep and other ranch animals graze. Colorado, however, is best known for its mountains, including the Rockies, which run through the center of the state. The state's rough natural setting is also the perfect backdrop for the National Western Rodeo, an annual sporting event that attracts thousands of tourists.

Hundreds of years before Europeans arrived, ancient people called the Anasazi built cliff dwellings of sandstone and mud in the canyons of southwestern Colorado. When Spanish explorers explored the area in the 1600s, they encountered Pawnee, Cheyenne, Arapaho, and Comanche, who lived in the flat plains areas, and the Ute, who lived in the mountain valleys. The Spaniards called the river that ran through the land *colorado*, Spanish for "red-colored." The state was named for the river.

In 1682, René-Robert Cavelier, Sieur de La Salle, claimed the land of eastern Colorado for France. Americans began exploring the area after 1803, when the U.S. bought eastern and central Colorado as part of the Louisiana Purchase. Mexico took over the western part of the state from Spain in 1821, only to have the U.S. gain control during the Mexican-American War. The Gold Rush in the late 1850s drew settlers to the area, leading to conflicts between settlers and the American Indians of the area.

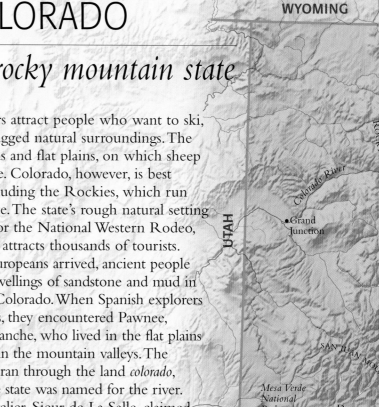

CLIFF DWELLINGS

The Cliff Palace is a complex in Mesa Verde National Park that contains 217 rooms and 23 kivas (underground ceremonial chambers). The sandstone and mud city was built in approximately A.D. 1000 by the Anasazi, an ancient people. The Anasazi moved to the area around A.D. 500 and lived in the cliffs before they carved out the city using riverbed stones.

RED CANYON ROCKS

Cropping up out of the red sandstone rocks west of downtown Denver is the open-air Red Rocks Amphitheater, where concerts are regularly held. The 9,000-seat venue was built inside a natural depression in the rock. It opened to the public in June of 1941. Red Rocks is nestled between two 400-foot (122-m) rocks that give off a unique red glow in the early morning and late evening as the sun and moon reflect off them. The rocky outcrop formed approximately 60 million years ago, and has red coloring due to its iron oxide content.

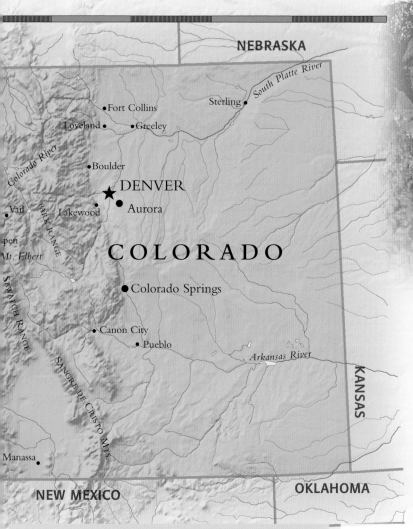

NEBRASKA

Fort Collins
Sterling
Loveland • Greeley
South Platte River

Colorado River
Boulder

DENVER
Vail
Lakewood • Aurora
pen
Mt. Elbert

COLORADO

• Colorado Springs

• Canon City
• Pueblo
Arkansas River

KANSAS

Manassa

NEW MEXICO OKLAHOMA

ROCKY MOUNTAIN HIGH

The Rocky Mountains are North America's biggest mountain system, extending from central New Mexico to northwestern Alaska. The range's largest peak, Mt. Elbert, is in Colorado. It stands 14,431 feet (4,307 m) high.

SKI COLORADO

Each year millions of tourists are drawn to Colorado's many winter resorts, such as Vail. Wintertime temperatures vary throughout Colorado. The western half is colder, dragging the state's average January temperature down to 28°F (-2°C). The average July temperature is 74°F (23°C).

BOXING LEGEND

WILLIAM HARRISON DEMPSEY

Nicknamed the Manassa Mauler in reference to his Colorado birthplace, William "Jack" Dempsey fought his way to become one of the U.S.'s most famous boxers in the 1920s. While in his teens, he won matches in saloons near Colorado's mining camps. Dempsey won his first professional fight in 1919 when he knocked out heavyweight champ Jess Willard seven times in three minutes.

Dempsey became heavyweight champion after his 1919 fight.

SHEEP RANCHING

Herds of sheep and beef cattle graze throughout Colorado's plains and mountains. The Great Plains covers the eastern two-fifths of the state, and is the state's main farming region. Crops, including sugar beets, hay, and corn, add to Colorado's agricultural income. The state's natural assets also include its mining industry.

RUGGED RODEO

Bucking broncos and rough-and-ready cowboys are a symbol of the rugged west and, thanks to rodeos, a form of entertainment in many western and southwestern states. The National Western Rodeo takes place each year in Denver, and features bull riding, barrel racing, and bronco riding. Denver is Colorado's largest city and a major economic force. It is the processing, shipping, and distribution center of Colorado's agricultural economy as well as the finance and business center of the Rocky Mountain region.

THE PACIFIC STATES

Calf-roping and bareback riding are just two of the events held at Oregon's annual Pendleton Round-Up, one of the largest rodeos in the nation.

Alaska, Hawaii, Oregon, Washington, and California have incredibly diverse climates, cultures, and settlement patterns—more so than any other region—but they share a proximity to the Pacific Ocean and its significant impact on their climate, economy, and culture.

Spanish explorers were the first to reach Washington, Oregon, and California, while the Russians and English were the first to reach Alaska and Hawaii, respectively.

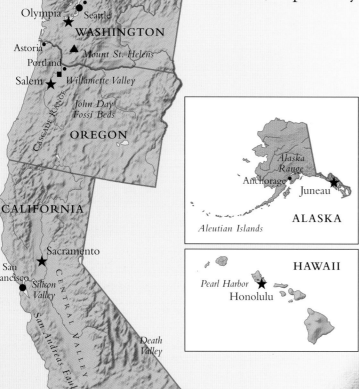

Gold played a decisive role in the settlement of the Pacific states. First discovered in the hills of California and Washington in the 1840s and 1850s, and in Alaska in the 1890s, it brought many eager to make their fortune. This settlement by whites meant forcible removal for American Indians such as the Nez Perce of Oregon's Pacific shore. The U.S. annexed Hawaii in 1898, in part because of its strategic location between Asia and North America. From the ice of Alaska's magnificent glaciers to the stars of Hollywood, the Pacific states make up a diverse and exciting region.

LANDSCAPE

The Pacific region is riddled with volcanic activity—undersea volcanoes formed both the Hawaiian Islands and Alaska's Aleutian Islands. More recently, Washington's Mount Saint Helens erupted in 1980. In Kimberly, Oregon, the John Day fossil beds have

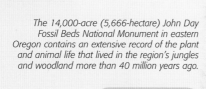

The 14,000-acre (5,666-hectare) John Day Fossil Beds National Monument in eastern Oregon contains an extensive record of the plant and animal life that lived in the region's jungles and woodland more than 40 million years ago.

KEY DATES

1805 The Lewis and Clark Expedition arrives at the Pacific Ocean, at what is today Astoria, Oregon.

1843 The first major wagon train, consisting of about 1,000 people, arrives in the Oregon territory via the Oregon Trail.

1862 Construction on the first transcontinental railroad is begun. When it is completed in 1869, California's population booms.

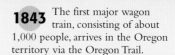

provided a record of plants and animals, preserved in volcanic deposits, dating back about 40 million years. California lies over two separate sections of the Earth's crust. The collision of these plates created the San Andreas Fault, which is prone to earthquakes. Southeastern California is primarily desert and home to Death Valley, which boasts the hottest recorded temperatures in the United States. The Alaskan and Cascade Ranges are among the many spectacular mountain chains found in the Pacific states.

CLIMATE

The climate of the Pacific states varies dramatically. Northernmost Alaska, located in the Arctic Circle, has average temperatures between –5°F and –20°F (–21°C and –29°C) in the winter months when there is little sunlight. Hawaii boasts a warm, tropical climate with 72° F (22° C) as an average winter temperature. Southern Alaska and the coastal regions of Washington, Oregon, and Northern California share a relatively mild climate with high levels of rainfall. Oregon, for example, averages up to 130 inches (330 cm) of precipitation per year with an average January temperature of 45°F (7°C). The desert regions of southern California are arid and receive only three to four inches (eight to 10 cm) of rain per year.

LIFESTYLE

The Pacific states include large Asian and Hispanic populations. Hawaii's native Polynesian culture remains vibrant through the Hawaiian language and customs. Much of the Pacific region is considered a vacation paradise, from the magnificent fjords and glaciers of coastal Alaska to the sandy beaches of southern California and Hawaii. The Pendleton Round-Up, established in Oregon in 1910, is a celebration of American Indian and U.S. cowboy culture complete, with bronco riding. Meanwhile, California has gained a reputation for a "laid-back" lifestyle and diverse culture.

First settled in 1851, Seattle experienced huge growth when the railroad reached it in 1893. Today, Seattle is a major metropolitan area of considerable natural beauty and a center for the aerospace and electronics industries.

Alaska's varied landscape includes more than 100,000 glaciers. The northern third of the state lies within the Arctic Circle.

ECONOMY

Important seaports, including San Diego, Los Angeles, Portland, Seattle, and San Francisco, line the Pacific Coast. These cities are the centers of commerce, industry, and trade in the region. Computer technology thrives in California's Silicon Valley and at Microsoft's headquarters in Redmond, Washington. The Willamette Valley in Oregon and the Central Valley in California have the region's top farmland. California leads the nation in agricultural output, producing grapes for wine and an astonishing range of fruits and vegetables. The forests of Oregon and Washington have made timber an important source of income. Alaska's bountiful natural resources make it a leading producer of oil, gold, and silver. Tourists flock to Hawaii to enjoy its tropical climate, scenic beauty, and exciting water sports; the processing of its harvest of sugarcane, pineapples, and coffee is this state's biggest industry.

California produces 97 percent of grapes grown in the United States. Farmers export one-third of their product to more than 50 countries around the world.

1867 The U.S. purchases Alaska from Russia. The Russians had first claimed the region in 1742.

1941 Japanese planes bomb Pearl Harbor, Hawaii. The U.S. declares war on Japan and enters World War II.

1977 The Trans-Alaska Pipeline System is completed. It carries oil more than 800 miles (1,287 km) across Alaska.

1980 Washington's Mount Saint Helens erupts. An estimated 10 million trees in the vicinity of the blast are destroyed.

STATE BIRD
Willow Ptarmigan

STATE FLOWER
Forget-me-not

STATE TREE
Sitka Spruce

CAPITAL
Juneau

POPULATION
626,932 (2000)

STATEHOOD
January 3, 1959
Rank: 49th

LARGEST CITIES
Anchorage (260,283)
Juneau (30,711)
Fairbanks (30,224)

LAND AREA
571,951 sq. mi.
(1,481,353 sq. km.)

ALASKA
land of the midnight sun

Glaciers, active volcanoes, forest-covered islands, massive fjords, tundra, snow-covered mountain peaks, polar bears, sea lions: all this and more can be found in Alaska, the nation's largest state and one of the richest in natural resources. Stretching from the Alaska Panhandle, the southernmost region bordering British Columbia, to the tundra, or arctic plains of the north, this region has a wide-ranging climate. Most major population centers are located within easy reach of its southern coastline on the Pacific Ocean.

The Haida of southern Alaska, the Eskimo of northwestern Alaska, and the Aleuts of the islands that bear their name, were the region's principle inhabitants before Europeans arrived. The state's name comes from the Aleutian word for "mainland" or "great land." Russians first came to Alaska in 1784 and controlled it until its sale to the United States in 1867.

In the twentieth century, exploitation of the region's natural resources, including the discovery of gold and then oil, has fueled the region's development. Today, Alaska remains a land of considerable natural resources and vast wilderness regions; the people of Alaska struggle to balance the demands of industry with conservation and preservation of the state's remarkable landscapes.

THE NORTHERN LIGHTS
Flashing bands of colored light appear in the Alaska sky when charged particles in outer space enter Earth's atmosphere. Most common in the summer months, when northern Alaska experiences 24 hours of daylight, this spectacular light show is also called the aurora borealis, Latin for "dawn of the north."

Aleutian Islands

Bering Sea

BLACK GOLD
Alaska's bountiful natural resources have long fueled the state's economy. The fur trade and fishing were the mainstays of its economy until gold was discovered. In the 1960s, the discovery of oil fields in the north led to the construction of the Trans-Alaska Pipeline System (TAPS). Completed in 1977, the pipeline is 800 miles (1,287 km) long and currently moves about one million barrels of oil each day.

PANNING FOR GOLD
In the 1890s, the discovery of gold in Canada's Yukon Territory, the region's eastern boundary, and then in Alaska itself brought an influx of fortune seekers; soon mining camps turned into bustling towns. Mining remains an important industry in the state, with gold, silver, lead, and zinc its leading products.

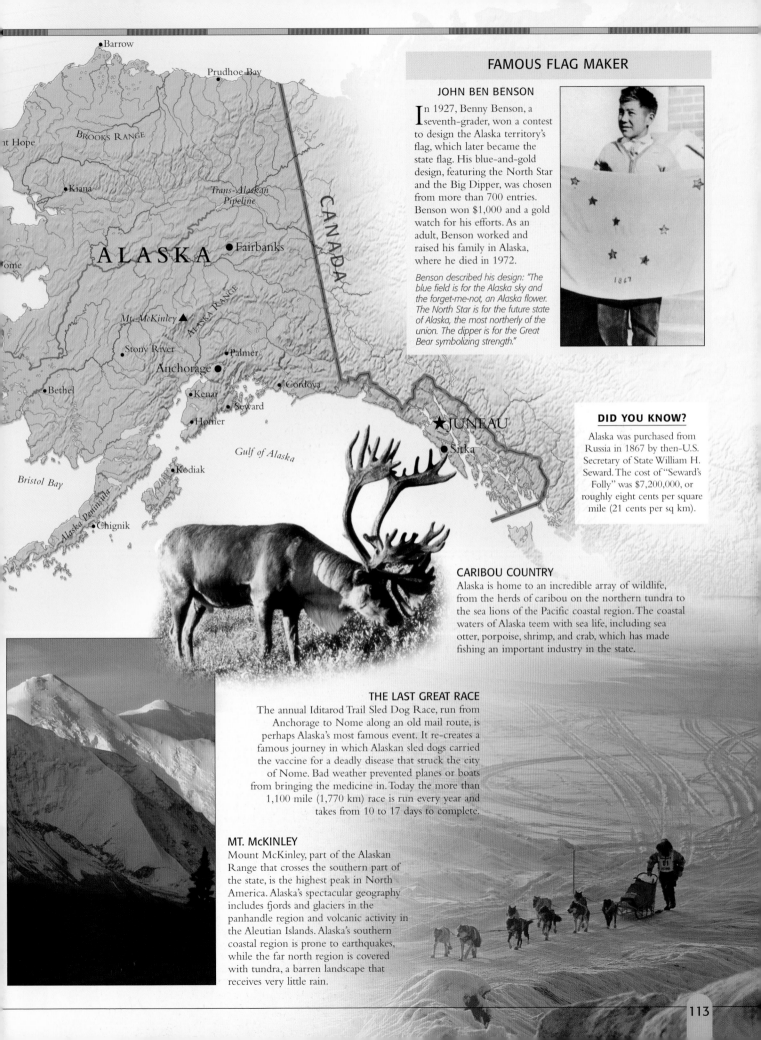

Barrow

Prudhoe Bay

BROOKS RANGE

t Hope

Kiana

Trans-Alaskan Pipeline

CANADA

ALASKA

Fairbanks

ALASKA RANGE

Mt. McKinley ▲

ome

Stony River

Palmer

Anchorage ●

Cordova

Bethel

Kenai

Seward

Homer

★JUNEAU

Gulf of Alaska

Sitka

Bristol Bay

Kodiak

Alaska Peninsula

Chignik

FAMOUS FLAG MAKER

JOHN BEN BENSON

In 1927, Benny Benson, a seventh-grader, won a contest to design the Alaska territory's flag, which later became the state flag. His blue-and-gold design, featuring the North Star and the Big Dipper, was chosen from more than 700 entries. Benson won $1,000 and a gold watch for his efforts. As an adult, Benson worked and raised his family in Alaska, where he died in 1972.

Benson described his design: "The blue field is for the Alaska sky and the forget-me-not, an Alaska flower. The North Star is for the future state of Alaska, the most northerly of the union. The dipper is for the Great Bear symbolizing strength."

DID YOU KNOW?

Alaska was purchased from Russia in 1867 by then-U.S. Secretary of State William H. Seward. The cost of "Seward's Folly" was $7,200,000, or roughly eight cents per square mile (21 cents per sq km).

CARIBOU COUNTRY

Alaska is home to an incredible array of wildlife, from the herds of caribou on the northern tundra to the sea lions of the Pacific coastal region. The coastal waters of Alaska teem with sea life, including sea otter, porpoise, shrimp, and crab, which has made fishing an important industry in the state.

THE LAST GREAT RACE

The annual Iditarod Trail Sled Dog Race, run from Anchorage to Nome along an old mail route, is perhaps Alaska's most famous event. It re-creates a famous journey in which Alaskan sled dogs carried the vaccine for a deadly disease that struck the city of Nome. Bad weather prevented planes or boats from bringing the medicine in. Today the more than 1,100 mile (1,770 km) race is run every year and takes from 10 to 17 days to complete.

MT. McKINLEY

Mount McKinley, part of the Alaskan Range that crosses the southern part of the state, is the highest peak in North America. Alaska's spectacular geography includes fjords and glaciers in the panhandle region and volcanic activity in the Aleutian Islands. Alaska's southern coastal region is prone to earthquakes, while the far north region is covered with tundra, a barren landscape that receives very little rain.

WASHINGTON
the evergreen state

STATE BIRD
Goldfinch

STATE FLOWER
Western Rhododendron

STATE TREE
Western Hemlock

CAPITAL
Olympia

POPULATION
5,894,121 (2000)

STATEHOOD
November 11, 1889
Rank: 42nd

LARGEST CITIES
Seattle (563,374)
Spokane (195,629)
Tacoma (193,556)

LAND AREA
66,544 sq. mi.
(172,349 sq. km.)

In 1775, Spanish explorers were the first Europeans to see Washington's shores; the British followed in 1792. In 1806, the first Americans arrived when Lewis and Clark's mapping expedition reached the Pacific Coast. At that time, many American Indian nations inhabited the Washington region, including the Spokane and Yakima, who lived on the plains and in river valleys east of the Cascade Mountains, while the Chinook and Puyallup lived on the range's western side.

American John Jacob Astor set up the first U.S. settlement at Fort Okanogan in order to take advantage of the rich furs available in the area. Meanwhile, England and the U.S. claimed the territory. Finally, in 1846, a treaty established the U.S.-Canada border.

Miners began settling in the area in 1860, while a railroad connection brought more settlers in 1883. When the U.S. entered World War I in 1917, Washington became the center of shipbuilding and forest products for the war effort. World War II brought aerospace and technology companies to the only state to be named for a U.S. president.

CLASHES WITH MISSIONARIES
Missionaries Marcus and Narcissa Whitman came to Oregon to preach Christianity among the Cayuse. After a measles epidemic killed 14 Cayuse in 1847, they attacked the mission, killing the Whitmans and 12 others.

RECORD NORTH AMERICAN VOLCANIC BLAST
An eruption on the north side of Mount St. Helens in the southwestern Cascade Range blasted stone, ash, and gases almost 20 miles (32 km) across the area on May 18, 1980. Dormant since 1857, the blast was one of the largest in North America's history.

NATIVE RESERVATIONS
This totem pole was carved from a tree called canoe cedar by American Indians of the Coastal Northwest. Washington is today home to 90,000 Indians, who live mainly on 27 reservations. The largest tribes are the Yakama on the Columbia Plateau in the east and the Lummi and Quinault in the west, while most other tribes have relatively small reservations.

GIANT OF THE AIR AND SPACE

The Boeing Company, a world leader in the production of commercial airliners and spacecraft, has headquarters in Seattle and large plants in Everett, Auburn, Kent, Renton, and Spokane. The Everett plant where 777 jets are built is the world's largest building.

ENJOY THE OUTDOORS

The Snake River, which separates Washington from Idaho, is prime for white-water rafting and kayaking. Washington's landscape also allows for skiing in the high mountains. The eastern section of the state has warmer summers and colder winters, while westerly winds from the Pacific ensure that winters in the west are relatively warm. The state's average temperatures range from 66°F (19°C) in July to 30°F (–1°C) in January.

THICK FORESTS BUILD ECONOMY

The state's nickname refers to its greatest natural resource: its forests. More than half of the state is forested; this resource has helped build the local economy historically and today. Many cities, including Tacoma and Everett, began as sawmill centers. Trees such as hemlock, which aren't strong enough for lumber, have been used to make pulp and paper products since the 1920s. Some trees in the central part of the state also yield plenty of apples, making Washington the country's leading apple supplier.

CANADA

Spokane ●

HINGTON

IDAHO

COLUMBIA PLATEAU

DID YOU KNOW?

The record for greatest annual snowfall in the U.S. is the 95 feet (29 m) that covered the Mount Baker Ski Area between July 1998 and June 1999.

CITY'S HIGH POINTS

Washington's largest city, Seattle, is also the largest city on the west coast north of San Francisco. Seattle's Pike Place Market is both a public market where locals shop for fresh fish and produce and a historic district that thousands of tourists visit each year. The market was founded in 1907 to help farmers who were not receiving fair prices for the crops they grew.

lumbia River

OREGON

COMPUTER GENIUS

WILLIAM HENRY GATES, III

At age 19, Bill Gates and partner Paul Allen left college to start Microsoft. In 1980, they began to develop an operating system for a personal computer for International Business Machines (IBM). That system, called Microsoft Disk Operating System (MS-DOS) and then Microsoft Windows, made Microsoft the world's largest microcomputer software producer. Today, Gates is chairman of Microsoft and one of the richest people in the world.

The Bill and Melinda Gates Foundation provides funds for education and health issues in developing countries.

STATE BIRD
Western Meadowlark

STATE FLOWER
Oregon Grape

STATE TREE
Douglas Fir

CAPITAL
Salem

POPULATION
3,421,399 (2000)

STATEHOOD
February 14, 1859
Rank: 33rd

LARGEST CITIES
Portland (529,121)
Eugene (137,893)
Salem (136,924)

LAND AREA
95,997 sq. mi.
(248,632 sq. km.)

OREGON
the beaver state

The Spanish were the first Europeans to visit Oregon's coast, in 1543. They were followed by English explorers and French fur traders, among others. In 1805, Meriwether Lewis and William Clark were the first Americans to cross the continent and reach Oregon's Pacific shore. The Chinook and Nez Perce peoples lived there at that time.

The origin of the state's name is unknown, but some historians believe it's named for the French word *ouragan*, which means "storm" or "hurricane," while more recent scholarship shows it may be derived from the Chinook word for fish oil, *ooligan*, which was traded among Oregon's Indians.

Throughout the late 1830s and 1840s, pioneers traveled across the country along the Oregon Trail. Today Oregon is known for its large forest areas, which cover half the state. In addition to mountains and forests, the state has a long seacoast. Among the state's beaches is Cannon Beach, which holds a festival called Sandcastle Day each year. In contrast, the fertile Willamette Valley is home to many farms that produce nursery plants and berries, among other items. Other unique settings that attract visitors to Oregon include the natural wonders of Painted Hills and Crater Lake National Park.

TRAIL'S END
The Oregon Trail was a pioneer route to the Pacific Coast in the 1830s and 1840s. The trail was created by mountain men such as James Bridger, who served as guides to settlers making the six-month journey. Oregon's fertile Willamette Valley was the main destination, and Oregon City was a popular stop. The trail was abandoned when the transcontinental railroad was completed.

INTERNMENT CAMPS
During World War II, President Roosevelt ordered all people of Japanese ancestry living west of the Cascade Mountains to leave their homes. In 1942, at least 110,000 West Coast Japanese and Japanese-Americans were moved into internment camps in eastern Oregon, California, Idaho, and Wyoming because the government feared that Japanese Americans might spy for Japan.

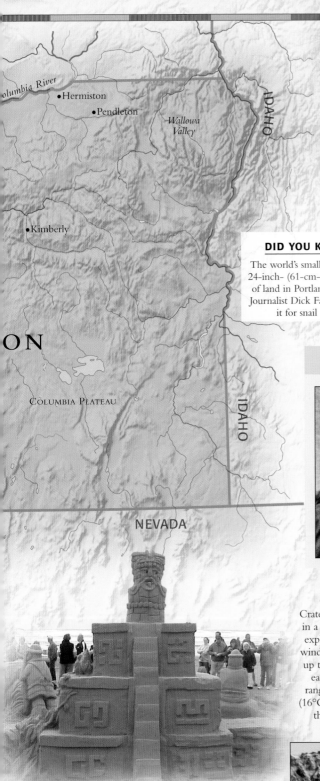

Columbia River
• Hermiston
• Pendleton

Wallowa Valley

IDAHO

• Kimberly

ON

COLUMBIA PLATEAU

IDAHO

NEVADA

PAINTED HILLS

Traces of life from 30 million years ago mark the colored rocks of Painted Hills, which contain wood and animal fossils as well as leaf prints. They are part of the John Day Fossil Beds and lie mainly in Kimberly, Oregon. The fossils formed after volcanic eruptions and include rare finds such as an ancient oak tree and the dawn redwood tree. The weather acted on the volcanic ash, causing rock layers to turn many colors.

"WE WILL FIGHT NO MORE FOREVER"

CHIEF JOSEPH

Chief Joseph was born in Oregon's Wallowa Valley around 1840. He became a Nez Perce leader in 1871. By 1877, Joseph's group and other American Indians faced forcible removal by the U.S. Army. Though they attempted to travel peaceably to an Idaho reservation, the army attacked them after officers were misinformed about their intentions. Chief Joseph and the other leaders attempted to lead his people to safety in Canada. Because Chief Joseph spoke on behalf of all native groups, he was held responsible for their actions.

When Chief Joseph surrendered, he made this now famous speech: "Our chiefs are dead, the little children are freezing. My people have no...food. From where the sun now stands, I will fight no more forever."

CRATER LAKE NATIONAL PARK

Crater Lake, the nation's second-deepest, lies in a pit formed when a prehistoric volcano exploded. Oregon benefits from the moist winds off the Pacific Ocean, which provides up to 130 inches (330 cm) of precipitation each year. Temperatures along the coast range from 45°F (7°C) in January to 60°F (16°C) in July, while the southeastern part of the state has much colder winters and warmer summers.

WILLAMETTE VALLEY

Agriculture is one of Oregon's biggest industries, and the Willamette Valley in the northwestern section of the state has become the center of production. The nutrient rich soil of the valley is the site of 70 percent of the state's farmland. Greenhouse and nursery plants are the state's main crop, bringing in more then $580 billion each year.

SANDCASTLE DAY

Each June, sandcastle lovers from around the world travel to Cannon Beach for one of the largest sand building contests on the West Coast. The contest began in 1964, after a tsunami washed out a local bridge and made travel difficult. Families gathered to take part in a sandcastle contest to entertain the children. Today, 150 teams compete to build structures out of sand and natural materials, such as seaweed and shells, and win awards. Castles are judged on form, as well as the building team's enthusiasm and cooperation. Each year, on the day before the event, sandsculpting classes are held at the beach.

STATE FACTS

STATE BIRD
California Quail

STATE FLOWER
Golden Poppy

STATE TREE
California Redwood

CAPITAL
Sacramento

POPULATION
33,871,648 (2000)

STATEHOOD
September 9, 1850
Rank: 31st

LARGEST CITIES
Los Angeles (3,694,820)
San Diego (1,223,400)
San Jose (894,943)

LAND AREA
155,959 sq. mi.
(403,934 sq. km.)

CALIFORNIA REPUBLIC

CALIFORNIA
the golden state

In 1542, Spanish explorer Juan Rodriguez Cabrillo became the first to record an exploration of northern California. At the time, approximately half a million American Indians, including the Shoshone and Chumash, lived along the Pacific Coast. Cabrillo named the land after a mythical island paradise featured in a sixteenth-century book, *Las Sergas de Esplandián*. Other European countries, including England, commissioned voyages to California, but few were eager to colonize the distant Pacific coast. More than 200 years later, in 1769, Father Junipero Serra opened the first of 21 Spanish missions in the region. Missions were churches established to convert Indians to Christianity and to cement Spain's control of the region.

In the mid- to late 1800s, gold was found in the Sierra Nevada mountains. Approximately 90,000 people went to California, hoping to get rich. Traveling to the area was difficult until the Transcontinental Railroad was completed in 1869.

Today, California's economy is larger than that of any other state.

It is also the most populous state and is visited by millions of tourists each year. California's generally sunny climate and mountain- and beach-lined coasts create a warm setting in which crops, particularly grapes, thrive.

GOLDEN GATE BRIDGE
The towering suspension bridge that spans San Francisco Bay was built in 1937 and measures 4,200 feet (1,280 m) long. The average walker takes half an hour to cross it. The bridge is San Francisco's symbol, as well as its focal point—it is visible from almost every high point in the city.

SCENIC VIEW
The view from Highway 1, part of California's much-traveled 1,200-mile (1,931 km) coastline, features the Pacific Ocean and a low-lying chain of mountains called the Coastal Ranges. Besides beaches, California has large areas of rolling hills, green or golden grasses, and thick forests. The warm, wet climate has helped some of the state's giant sequoia trees reach more than 300 feet (91 m) tall. Giant sequoias mainly grow high in the mountains, while many coast redwoods line the seashore on the California/Oregon border at Redwood National Park.

CHINESE NEW YEAR
Each February, the Chinese New Year is celebrated in grand style throughout the 24 blocks that make up San Francisco's Chinatown. California's Chinatown is the second largest Chinese community outside of Asia. Many Chinese immigrants settled in San Francisco after working on the Transcontinental Railroad.

Map labels: Crescent City, Klamath, Eureka, Redding, Fort Bragg, Chico, Ukiah, Citrus Heights, SACRAMENTO, Santa Rosa, Napa, Concord, Stockton, Berkeley, Oakland, San Francisco, Fremont, Sunnyvale, San Jose, Salinas, Monterey, COAST RANGES

NAPA AND SONOMA VALLEYS

Due to a long growing season, rich soils, and sunny skies, the rolling hills and valleys of Sonoma and Napa produce California's finest wines. Their 29,000 acres (11,736 ha) of grape vines, used almost solely for wine making, are among the state's most valuable assets.

HOME OF HOLLYWOOD

The Hollywood sign, which was originally a real-estate ad, announces that visitors have arrived in the world's entertainment capital. The 460-square-mile (1,191-sq-km) city of Los Angeles, which includes Hollywood, has sandy beaches, a busy shipping port, and tall metropolitan buildings built to withstand the earthquakes that occasionally rock the area.

NEVADA

Yosemite National Park

SIERRA NEVADA

CALIFORNIA DREAMIN'

California's coastline is 1,200 miles (1,931 km) long. All that coast makes for a lot of beach. Among the most famous of the state's beaches are those at Malibu in Southern California. There people swim, sun, and surf throughout the year, thanks to California's warm climate.

esno

Visalia

DEATH VALLEY RECORD HIGH

In 1913, the temperature in the Death Valley desert reached 134°F (57°C), the hottest on record in the U.S. Less than two inches (five cm) of rain falls here annually, but that is enough for a variety of small animals and desert plants. California's diverse landscape, which includes snow-topped mountains, forests, and deserts, makes the state's average temperatures seem extreme, but July's average is 75°F (24°C) while January's is 44°F (7°C).

DEATH VALLEY

CALIFORNIA

Bakersfield

COAST RANGES

Santa Barbara

Lancaster

Hesperia

Glendale

Los Angeles

Oxnard

Malibu   Santa Monica

Long Beach   Cypress

CIFIC OCEAN

Oceanside   Escondido

San Diego

ARIZONA

GOLF'S YOUNGEST MASTER

ELDRICK "TIGER" WOODS

This native of Cypress, California, began practicing his golf swing well before his second birthday. Woods played his first professional tournament in 1992, and by 2002, he had won 45 tournament titles. His 1997 Masters win made him the youngest ever Masters champion and the first of African and Asian heritage. When he won his second Masters title in 2001, Woods became the first golf player ever to hold all four of golf's professional title championships at the same time.

By age 16, Woods was a six-time international champion.

DID YOU KNOW?

The world's tallest tree stands in Ukiah, California. This coast redwood, also called a sequoia, is nearly 368 feet (112 m) tall.

MEXICO

STATE FACTS

STATE BIRD
Nene (Hawaiian Goose)

STATE FLOWER
Yellow Hibiscus

STATE TREE
Kukui (Candlenut)

CAPITAL
Honolulu

POPULATION
1,211,537 (2000)

STATEHOOD
August 21, 1959
Rank: 50th

LARGEST CITIES
Honolulu (371,657)
Hilo (40,759)
Kailua (36,513)

LAND AREA
6,423 sq. mi.
(16,636 sq. km.)

HAWAII
the aloha state

The 137 Hawaiian islands, 8 of which are inhabited, were probably first settled by Polynesians from Southeast Asia, who sailed across the Pacific Ocean around A.D. 750. The Polynesians named the island chain, although it is unknown if they named it after the islands' discoverer, Chief Hawai'i-loa, or after their homeland of Hawaiki.

English explorer Captain James Cook became the first European to visit the islands in 1778. By 1810, ruler Kamehameha I had encouraged the adoption of Western systems, including trading for profit. Missionaries began visiting the islands in 1820 and helped to establish schools.

The U.S. government developed an interest in the islands's sugar trade and its locale. In 1887, the U.S. established exclusive rights to create a naval base at Pearl Harbor on the island of Oahu. In 1893, Americans involved in the sugar industry encouraged an overthrow of the islands's last monarch, Queen Liliuokalani, and Hawaii was annexed by the U.S. in 1898. During this time, the island's pineapple industry grew. By the time Hawaii became a state, its economy was thriving. Hawaii is now a major producer of fruit products and a year-round playground for those who love water sports.

SWEET SUCCESS
Pineapples and sugarcane, the plant from which sugar is produced, are Hawaii's main agricultural products. They are the basis for the state's biggest industry—food processing. The production of sugar, pineapple juice, and fruit products brought in $276.1 million in 1999.

NIIHAU

Mt. Kilauea

KAUAI

NATIVE DANCE
With their gently swaying hips and smooth hand gestures, hula dancers look as if they are communicating—and they are. The dance, first performed hundreds of years ago as part of a religious service, is meant to communicate stories or future events. The hula, a Hawaiian word that means "dance" is accompanied by music often played on steel guitars and ukeleles, small guitars with four strings.

VACATION PARADISE
With a bright, Pacific setting, sunny, moderately humid climate, gentle cool breezes, and world-famous beaches, it's no wonder tourism is Hawaii's main income source. The land that Mark Twain once described as the "loveliest fleet of islands that lies anchored in any ocean" receives visitors from around the world, including those who enjoy surfing and other sports in and out of the water. In 2000 alone, Hawaii welcomed 6,948,595 tourists. These guests spent $10.9 billion, proving that tourism and the service industry are big business.

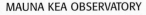

ROYAL LAST STAND

QUEEN LILIUOKALANI

Lydia Liliuokalani was Hawaii's first queen and final royal ruler. She came to the throne at age 53 upon the death of her brother, King Kalakaua, in 1891. In part, her reign ended when sugar planters, mostly U.S. citizens living on Hawaii, grew angry that she was determined to stop the U.S. from gaining control. In January 1893, a small group of Americans and Europeans joined the U.S. Marines in taking Liliuokalani out of power. Two years later, after failing to reclaim her royal title, she ended her fight.

Liliuokalani wrote more than 150 songs, including her most famous, "Aloha Oe."

ACTIVE VOLCANOES

Hawaii's most active volcano is on the big island of Hawaii. Mt. Kilauea has been blowing burning lava sky-high regularly since 1983. Two other volcanoes, Mauna Loa and Loihi are also currently active. Erupting volcanoes have always been common sites around Hawaii. In fact, the islands are the result of volcanic activity. Thousands of years ago, undersea volcanoes burst 15,000 feet up from the ocean floor. Many of them cooled off and became gently sloping mountains on which people could live.

OAHU

★HONOLULU

Pearl Harbor

HAWAII

MOLOKAI

PACIFIC OCEAN

Lanai

•Kailua

MAUI

Kahoolawe

DID YOU KNOW?

Hawaii is the only state to have two official languages: English and Hawaiian.

PEARL HARBOR

At 7:55 A.M. on December 7, 1941, Japanese planes dropped bombs on the U.S. naval base at Pearl Harbor in Oahu, Hawaii. After almost two hours of attacks, Pearl Harbor was a wreck. At least 2,335 servicemen and 68 civilians were killed and 188 planes and 18 ships were destroyed on the once-peaceful island. The next day, President Franklin Roosevelt declared the U.S. would enter World War II to combat Japan. Pearl Harbor is still used as a naval shipyard.

▲
Mauna Kea

•Hilo

HAWAII

MAUNA KEA OBSERVATORY

The world's largest astronomical observatory stands on Mauna Kea Peak. Owned by the University of Hawaii's Institute for Astronomy, the Mauna Kea Observatory is home to the world's most famous telescopes. The largest are the 33-foot-tall (10-m-) W. M. Keck telescopes, called Keck I and Keck II, which provide amazingly detailed images of the universe.

STATE BIRD
Wood Thrush

STATE FLOWER
American Beauty Rose

STATE TREE
Scarlet Oak

POPULATION
572,059 (2000)

GOVERNMENT BRANCHES

EXECUTIVE BRANCH
President

LEGISLATIVE BRANCH
Congress

JUDICIAL BRANCH
Supreme Court

LAND AREA
68 sq. mi
(177 sq. km)

WASHINGTON, D.C.

our nation's capital

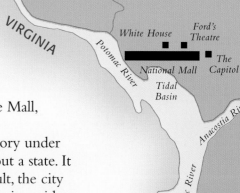

WASHINGTON, D.C.

VIRGINIA

Potomac River

White House

Ford's Theatre

National Mall

The Capitol

Tidal Basin

Anacostia River

Potomac River

VIRGINIA

Both Maryland and Virginia gave up land for the creation of the new seat of the U.S. government, but the city was built only on that land formerly belonging to Maryland. The district, named for Christopher Columbus, was established in 1790 as the United States's national capital. In 1871, it was consolidated into the city of Washington, D.C., named in honor of the nation's first president.

Designed to impress visitors from home and abroad, Washington, D.C., is a city of grand monuments to important leaders and events in U.S. history. Many of these monuments are located on the Mall, which is also the site of the Washington Monument. Washington, D.C.'s unique situation as a federal territory under the direct control of Congress has made it city without a state. It does not have Congressional representatives. As a result, the city has suffered severe financial problems over the years as its residents and elected officials have struggled to get funding from Congress for transportation and physical improvements, as well as adequate schools and housing.

Today Washington, D.C., is a thriving metropolitan center that draws workers from the public and private sector and visitors from around the world who enjoy the considerable political, social, and cultural benefits of life in the nation's capital.

THE PEACEFUL POTOMAC

The Potomac River flows through Washington, D.C., providing much natural beauty, a thriving river ecosystem, and a site for water-based recreation and sport. The city is located where the Potomac and Anacostia Rivers meet along the southern border of Maryland and the northern border of Virginia. The city was initially built on land that was primarily mosquito-infested swamp and marshland that drove early inhabitants away in the summer months. Drainage and development has since created a bustling metropolitan area with hot, humid summers and damp, chilly winters.

A TRAGIC EVENT

President Abraham Lincoln's visit to see *Our American Cousin* at Ford's Theatre ended in tragedy on April 14, 1865, when he was shot by John Wilkes Booth, a former actor and Confederate sympathizer. Lincoln was taken to Petersen House, a boardinghouse across the street, where he died the next morning. The theater and boardinghouse today commemorate the life and untimely death of one of the nation's greatest leaders.

THE HOME OF PRESIDENTS

In 1800, John Adams became the first president to occupy what was then known as the Executive Mansion. It was the first public building constructed in the nation's new capital. During the War of 1812, the British set fire to it—First Lady Dolley Madison saved some of the nation's treasures from the burning building. At the war's end, the structure needed substantial reconstruction. The classically designed building became officially known as the White House in 1901, during Theodore Roosevelt's presidency. Tours of the formal state rooms of the home and workplace of America's chief executive are open to the public, and it is the most-visited home in the nation.

MARYLAND

DID YOU KNOW?

D.C. residents couldn't vote in presidential elections until 1964. A Constitutional amendment was required to give Washingtonians their rights. The 23rd Amendment was passed in 1960 and ratified in 1961.

HOMETOWN BEAT

CONNIE CHUNG

Today Connie Chung works as a news anchor for CNN.

Journalist Connie Chung, a native of Washington, D.C., is among a select group of women who have broken into the top ranks of network television news broadcasting. From 1993 to 1995 she served as co-anchor of the CBS Evening News, becoming the second woman ever to have served in the anchor's chair. Chung has worked for all the major networks and hosted many network news programs, covering many issues, including presidential campaigns, international peace talks, and the AIDS crisis. This award-winning reporter exemplifies the spirit of public service.

SENATE IN SESSION

The U.S. Senate, one of the two houses of the legislative branch of government, is one of the many governmental bodies that meet in Washington, D.C. Judges, lawyers, and others are also employed by the federal government. In addition, the city is home to lobbyists and foreign diplomats. Many national and international organizations have Washington offices. Each year, millions of visitors come to the city to tour the Capitol Building and other monuments, making tourism an important source of revenue.

HIGH-FLYERS

In the spring when the cherry blossoms are in full bloom beside Washington's Tidal Basin, the Smithsonian Kite Festival is held on the lawn of the Mall. Sponsored by the National Air and Space Museum, the festival draws kite fliers from around the world. This celebration of aviation illustrates the brilliance of the city's design, which incorporates informal, green spaces in the midst of awe-inspiring monuments.

OUTLYING REGIONS

The U.S. controls four self-governing island territories: Puerto Rico, the U.S. Virgin Islands, American Samoa, and Guam. In 1898, after the Spanish-American War, Spain ceded Puerto Rico and Guam to the U.S. Guam became a territory in 1950; Puerto Rico voluntarily became associated with the United States in 1952. The U.S. Virgin Islands, located in the Caribbean, and American Samoa, in the South Pacific, formally became territories in 1917 and 1929 respectively. These regions provide both markets for U.S. goods and sites for U.S. military installations.

BOUNTIFUL HARVEST
Sugarcane is Puerto Rico's major crop. Plantains, bananas, and other tropical fruits are also important products. Tourism generates considerable income, given the island's tropical climate and considerable natural beauty.

PUERTO RICO

The island of Puerto Rico was claimed by Spain in 1493, and was ruled by the Spanish until 1898. *Puerto Rico* means "rich port" in Spanish. Puerto Rico has been a U.S. territory since 1898. It has held plebiscites, or popular votes, in 1967, 1993, and 1998. Each time, voters have chosen not to become the 51st U.S. state.

ATLANTIC OCEAN

San Juan

Caribbean Sea

CROSS-POLLINATION
Spanish, American, African, and Caribbean influences have created a vibrant cultural life, reflected in the distinctive food, music, dance, and language of Puerto Rico. Today more than three million Puerto Ricans have emigrated to the U.S. and live throughout the nation.

EL MORRO CASTLE
Spanish explorers, the first of whom was Christopher Columbus, encountered the Taino people living on Puerto Rico. El Morro Castle, located in the present-day capital of San Juan, was one of several forts built by the Spanish in the early 1500s to defend their growing colonial empire in North and South America. Coffee, sugarcane, and tobacco plantations flourished in the tropical climate of Puerto Rico in the 1800s and made the island a valuable asset when the United States seized control during the Spanish-American War in 1898.

UNITED STATES VIRGIN ISLANDS

The U.S. Virgin Islands, purchased from Denmark in 1917 for $25 million, consist of the major islands of St. Croix, St. John, and St. Thomas as well as numerous cays and islets. Today the islands host more than two million visitors each year, accounting for 70 percent of the region's revenue.

ISLAND PARADISE
A tropical climate and beautiful scenery has made the islands a popular vacation and retirement destination. Farming and food processing also play a dynamic role in the islands' economy.

AMERICAN SAMOA

These islands, located in the South Pacific, were first acquired by the U.S in the late 1800s in order to build a naval base at Pago Pago. American Samoa consists of seven islands, five of which are inhabited.

VOLCANIC ISLANDS
American Samoa has been occupied by Polynesians since as early as 1000 B.C. The Polynesian peoples are thought to have originated in Australia and populated many islands, including Hawaii. Here Samoans row their traditional boat, which is used for fishing. Today the coconut harvest, tuna canning, and tourism fuel Samoa's economy.

GUAM

Guam boasts a diverse population comprised of the Chamarro (its indigenous people), Americans, Chinese, Japanese, and others. Today it is home to Andersen Air Force Base, one of the most important U.S. bases in the South Pacific.

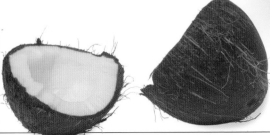

COCONUT
Coconuts, sugarcane, and poultry are leading agricultural products on this volcanic Pacific island, which also boasts an oil refinery and textile plants. Tourism is an important industry, too.

ANDERSEN AIR FORCE BASE
Japan occupied Guam during World War II, leading to a major U.S. assault to regain control on August 10, 1944. Guam then became the site of major U.S. military installations, including Andersen Air Force Base. The U.S. military owns about one-third of the land.

INDEX

126

The author and DK Publishing, Inc. offer their grateful thanks to: MacAllister Publishing Services for the state bird, flower, and tree illustrations and Rob Stokes for the state maps.